STREET HAWK™*
annual 1986
TOP
BOT
LS
RS
FR
RR
SYS MON
BEAM LEVEL
£ 3.25

Contents

Licensed by Merchandising Corporation of America, Inc.
Published in Great Britain by
World International Publishing Limited
P.O. Box 111, Great Ducie Street, Manchester M60 3BL.
Printed in Italy. SBN 7235 6759 X.

BAD APPLES

As the taxi nosed slowly onto the second storey of the car park, the driver peered at the other cars standing motionless in the gloom, then turned to his passenger in the back. "You sure your car's on this floor, mister?" he asked.

"I'm not exactly sure. Maybe it was the third floor."

The taxi driver shrugged and headed for the ramp. Behind him, muscular hands uncoiled a short length of plastic rope.

"You said it was a grey Porsche, right?" the taxi driver inquired as the cab slid onto the third storey.

"Right," the man agreed, suddenly leaning forward, looping the rope round the driver's neck, then pulling back hard. "But I forgot to tell you I was lying!" The taxi driver clawed at the rope round his neck with one hand as the other pounded the cab's horn. He grabbed for the door but the man behind held him back, tightening his grip all the time. The coarse plastic twine was cutting off the driver's air supply and he felt the chill grey hand of oblivion closing slowly round his senses when – completely without warning – there was a flash of brilliant white light from behind, the chamber echoed to the urgent, high-powered scream of supercharged engines and, after the strange hissing of vertical lift compressed air thrusters had passed over the roof of the cab, a sleek black motorcycle crashed to the ground ahead of them, spun round and stopped, its single blinding headlamp freezing the ugly scene.

The rider, unrecognisable in his jet black outfit, stood astride the purring monster like an avenging demon.

"S-S-Street Hawk!" gasped the would-be mugger, letting go of the rope. "I gotta get out of here!" The taxi driver was gratefully rubbing his neck as the thug kicked open the back door and made a run for it down the ramp.

On the high-tech turbo-designed motorcycle, Jesse Mach – sometime low-profile PR man with the police department, sometime street crime fighter supreme – swivelled the snub barrel of his laser particle beam gun, set it for stun, and opened fire. Wriggling, crackling bolts of pure blue energy leaped from the stationary bike, hitting the fleeing thug square in the back and knocking him to the ground. Jesse nodded briefly to the rescued cabbie then, with another deep-throated roar from his supercycle's mighty engines, raced off down the ramp and into the night.

Back at the command centre, Federal Government Research Engineer Norman Tuttle, builder of the three million dollar motorcycle, smiled at the performance of his creation.

"A bit too much showboating, Jesse," he said over the communicator, as he studied the pictures relayed by the bike's cameras. "But all systems appear to be in perfect working order."

"You said it, Norman," agreed Jesse, sliding the low-slung speedster round Hollywood and Vine. "My little baby's really cooking tonight."

Norman grimaced at Jesse's choice of words and punched the hyperthrust countdown into his computer. "You ready to check the turbos?"

Jesse tightened his grip on the speeding motorcycle. "Ready." He nodded. Inside his helmet he watched the speedo hold steady at 50 mph as the countdown went on,

steadying himself against the sudden exhilarating burst of spine-tingling naked power he knew would erupt when Norman cut in the turbos and the hyperthrust shot them forward like a bullet from a gun.

"5 . . . 4 . . . 3 . . . 2 . . ."

"Norman! Hold it! Cancel hyperthrust! I think I see something!"

Norman stopped the countdown and studied the screen. Some 200 metres ahead of Jesse, a large black truck was slowly lowering its tailgate. As Norman zoomed in on the licence plate, Jesse cruised along behind. His suspicions grew when two trail bikes slid down the ramp and, after the truck had made a sharp right, they expertly moved up fast on another van directly ahead. Jesse recognised it as one of the supposedly unmarked and inconspicuous vehicles the government had provisionally adopted for the transportation of gold bullion.

"Highway robbery," said Jesse into his mike. "Going down right now."

"I see it. Am checking for clearance."

Jesse kept his distance as the two bikes hugged the van's tail. He knew there would be some kind of back-up for the shipment, but apart from a lone black and white leading the van through the darkened streets, he couldn't see any. Then the two cyclists speeded up and Jesse saw them lean across from their bikes and place small square metal boxes just above the spinning wheels. They dropped back, stuck two more above the locks on the thick metal door, then peeled off down a sidestreet.

"Some kind of magnetic explosive. I'm going after them."

"Not yet, Jesse," ordered Norman. "I'm still awaiting clearance."

Suddenly, as the lone black and white passed over a manhole, the ground shook with a tremendous shuddering boom and a yellow blast of heat and flame soared up from the blown manhole cover, lifting the car and its occupants into the air. As the two officers inside dived under the dashboard for safety, the black and white spiralled gracefully, silently turning under the garish yellow streetlights, before it slammed down onto the road with the harsh sound of smashing glass and grinding, tearing, tortured metal. The roof caved in, the lights were crushed and the sirens squashed, and the devastated squad car skidded noisily upside down across an intersection, flipped up on its shredded front wheels when it rear-ended an imported British sports car, hung crazily upright for a few seconds, then flopped slowly down with its chassis across the sports car's empty, open front seats.

Before Jesse had time to check the policemen, the bombs on the van went off. Two sharp blasts of fire took out the back wheels and as the van slewed sideways into the intersection the two at the back blew the doors wide open. The two motorcyclists reappeared at speed,

Norman's voice suddenly adopted a pleading conciliatory note. "Jesse, please. I ran their plate through the computer. You've got to trust me. This is Federal business."

"Attacking cops is Federal business?" Jesse's voice expressed his astonishment.

Norman continued his explanation. "The cops are agents too. It's a STING operation, Jesse – a set-up to catch much bigger fish. You'll louse the whole thing up if you bring them in."

Jesse gunned the revs as the cyclists roared off in different directions and the black truck lumbered down the main drag, its suspension creaking under the weight of its booty. The two cops clambered unsteadily from the wreck of their car and the truck turned a corner out of sight.

"I may not be able to bring them in," observed Jesse, setting off in pursuit, "but I'm sure going to find out where they're going."

Jesse tailed the slow-moving truck through the night, barely tapping the awesome resources of his sleek, fast machine. The infra-red cameras told him there were three men in the vehicle, and when they finally stopped and got out at a disused airfield out of town, his night vision identified at least two of them as high-level members of Mike Lomax's gang of racketeers. With growing frustration he watched as an unmarked Bell Long Ranger helicopter drifted down from the lightening skies like a mammoth mechanical insect and put down by the truck. As the gold was being loaded the infra-red identified a single pilot at the controls.

"Last chance to slam the door on these yo-yos," he reminded Norman.

"Nix, Jesse," Norman replied. "We obey the KEEP OFF sign. It's time to come home."

And as the fully laden chopper swung up through a cloud of dust into the clear morning air, Jesse bit back his anger and turned the

and were covering the driver with handguns while the black truck that had once housed them backed up to the stricken bullion van. As three men climbed out and began loading up gold, Jesse hit the button and the stubby barrels of the high energy particle beam gun clicked quietly into position. Inside his helmet he saw the targetting system lock on the truck's motor.

"Targetting locked," he said grimly, preparing to fire. "Those bozos are all mine."

"Negative, Mach," said Norman urgently. "Mission aborted. You are not cleared for encounter. Repeat – you are not cleared for encounter!"

"Can it, Norm – I'm taking these babies off the streets!" Through the nerve-centre of the super-sophisticated helmet, both Norman and Jesse could see the thieves had almost finished transferring the gold to the truck.

"This is an order, Mach. Let them go or I'll cut your power."

"These punks attacked a police car. I'm taking them in."

high-performance motorcycle back towards the command centre.

"This is all strictly confidential," Norman explained, after Jesse had been debriefed. "We have a man in Lomax's gang. He's been lying low for years, risking his life to gain Lomax's trust. He told us that Lomax planned to steal the bullion and have it relayed to his yacht outside territorial waters. The Coast Guard was waiting there to catch him red-handed with the loot."

"Maybe I underestimated you guys. That's a pretty smart plan."

Norman looked embarrassed. He coughed uneasily. "It would have been a smart plan," he agreed, "if the chopper with the bullion on board hadn't exploded two miles out to sea."

"What?" asked Jesse in amazement.

"The chopper went down with our man on board. Some agents on a fishing boat saw the whole thing – they've just reported in."

"You got a profile of your man?" asked Jesse.

Norman hesitated.

"Are we partners or not?" Jesse persisted.

Norman shook his head wryly as he punched the computer buttons. The name Ralph Meeker appeared above a photograph of an athletic-looking middle-aged man. Below the picture, his impressive list of achievements included a degree in engineering, a wide knowledge of explosives and an exemplary record as a helicopter pilot in South East Asia.

"You know him?" asked Jesse.

Norman nodded. "We studied together on some projects. He was a very good engineer."

"Good enough to rig up a remote control system that could take an unmanned Bell Long Ranger two miles out to sea?"

"Now hold on there, Mach," Norman complained, jumping angrily to his feet. "The man gave his life fighting crime."

"What time did the chopper go down?"

"You're crazy, Jesse," said Norman, working the buttons again.

Jesse looked over his shoulder. "7.49!" he exclaimed as the numbers came up. "I saw him fly off just before seven. That gave him plenty of time to unload the gold, set the chopper on course then bale out. One medium sized bomb with an electronic timer and –"

"You're losing your marbles, Mach. Meeker was a perfect company man, happily married . . ."

"His wife," Jesse interrupted. "Where is she now?"

"She'll be in shock, of course. There's an agent at her house right now."

"Contact him."

"I can't do that. The poor woman –"

"I didn't say contact the woman – I asked you to contact your man."

"But –"

"You want to keep the company clean, don't you?"

"Sure I do, but –"

"Do it."

Norman paced the room for several seconds then sat down by the phone and dialled. His face became puzzled as he listened. "Static," he said, holding the mouthpiece up in the palm of his hand. "Nothing but static."

"You said it, buster," Jesse barked as he picked up his helmet and pulled it on. "And I think it's time we made a connection."

Within minutes, the camouflaged doors to the secret command centre slid open and the jet black, turbo-designed supercycle rocketed from its lair like a startled thoroughbred, landed with its wheels spinning, and screeched off towards Mrs Meeker's house.

When he arrived at Mrs Meeker's white wooden bungalow it seemed Jesse's hunch had been wrong. The place was quiet, and in the garden next door an old man was happily watering his plants. And then the infra-red picked up a body in the hallway. A body that was rapidly losing its body heat. Jesse hit the particle beam controls and the flickering blue bolts of energy snaked out, fizzing and crackling round the front door frame until suddenly the hinges gave way and the oak door tumbled out. It crunched beneath the wheels of the attack motorcycle as Jesse rode into the hall.

"Ambulance on its way," said Norman.

Jesse dismounted and knelt over the injured agent. A dark stain on his light grey suit told Jesse he'd been shot. As Jesse tried to make the man comfortable, he suddenly opened his eyes. "Airport . . . Meeker . . . airport . . ."

Jesse waited until he heard the ambulance siren approaching, then rode his gleaming two-wheeled partner into the street. Norman had already started the countdown to hyperthrust on the computer assist mode.

"3 . . . 2 . . . 1 . . . You got it!"

The turbos ignited and Jesse clung on as the thundering motors made full use of the mean machine's miniscule aerodynamic drag co-efficient of 0.05, accelerating onto the freeway until the speed monitor on the top left hand corner of his helmet read 300 mph.

"Hyperthrust achieved," said Norman calmly, plotting the route to the airport.

"You'd better believe it," muttered Jesse as cars, vans and lorries were left behind in a continuous blue of speed and action. "You checked departures?"

"Sure. We got a probable on the next flight to Rio. It takes off in three minutes."

"I'm going over the fence."

"Jesse . . ." But Norman didn't bother. He knew it was too late to back out now. As the airport loomed closer he disengaged hyperthrust, and when Jesse cut in the air foils to take full advantage of the negative air flow, he sat back to watch the action.

Jesse raced across an open stretch of road and as the perimeter fence came hurtling towards him, activated the compressed air vertical lift system. The jets hissed angrily and the sleek speedster jumped the fence and surged along the runway, where a Boeing 747 was warming up for its take-off run.

"Jesse!" Norman shouted in alarm. "You can't –"

"You never know what you can do till you try."

Jesse pulled alongside the 747 as the massive jet's gigantic 20 tonne-plus engines screamed in protest at the pilot building up the revs to maximum. Jesse hit the compressed air button again and his speeding supercycle, dwarfed by the shuddering giant, leaped from the tarmac onto the wing.

In the command centre, Norman looked away from the screen.

"Mommy," said a small boy in the window seat of the 747, "there's a man on a motorcycle on the wing."

Even as the young boy spoke, Jesse gunned the accelerator, cut in the compressed air to jump the wide body and skidded along the other wing, stopping, rearing up and turning on one wheel at the tip of the 195 foot wingspan. When he repeated the manoeuvre the pilot began getting strange messages from the tower. The puzzled airman couldn't make out exactly what the flight controllers were trying to tell him, but the meaning was clear. Take off was postponed.

"He's there again, Mom," the boy persisted. "He's doing wheelies. I think it's Street Hawk."

"Yes, dear," his mother said distractedly as the sudden loss of power in the engines made her look up from her diet book. Behind her, a furious shouting match was developing between Mrs Meeker and her crooked husband. The boy watched eagerly as Jesse cut in the air jets again, hopped off the Boeing's wing and accelerated away towards the perimeter fence. The world's most expensive motorbike jumped the fence, and when Norman cut in the hyperthrust, it disappeared into the distance in seconds.

"Now then," said Mother, leaning over. "What's all this about a bird?"

The boy gazed across the deserted wing at the spot where the bike had finally pulled out of sight.

"Nothing, Mom," he sighed.

For Jesse Mach, in his PR job for a police force under close media scrutiny, the answers wouldn't be quite that simple.

THE COILS of the COBRA

"Sorry to interrupt you when you're so hard at work," Jesse Mach heard a voice say as a hand grasped the top of the sports section and the newspaper he was reading was whisked from his grasp. As the column of newsprint disappeared, Jesse found himself staring across his desk at Sandy's smiling face. "I've got a date for you – Rita Henderson. I've just been watching her work on the TV."

"On the TV?" repeated Jesse questioningly as he snatched back his newspaper and put it down on his desk beside an empty plastic cup. "Don't tell me – she stars in an afternoon soap and you met her on a computer doubledate. When you found out she had a thing for ex-motorcycle cops you naturally thought of me. Right?"

"Not even close," said Sandy. "Miss Henderson makes a living asking people awkward questions in front of a TV camera. Right now she wants to know exactly where the department stands on the Ernie Noguera case."

Ernie Noguera had started as a chippie then gone on to become a detective with the department. He had still retained his enthusiasm for motorcycles even after his promotion, and three weeks ago he had been killed when a Honda he had been riding slid from under him in the wet when he braked to avoid a dog that had run out into the road. Since his death, evidence had come to light that linked him to a series of hold-ups that had taken place in small town banks throughout Southern California, and somehow the media had got hold of the information concerning this investigation before it had been completed.

"Why pick me to do the 'spokesperson for the department said' routine?" asked Jesse. "Don't you know this is personal? Ernie and me were cycle cops together. I'm a friend of the family."

"That's exactly why Altobelli wants you to talk to her. He can rely on you to use your judgment because of it. Rita Henderson has a way of provoking her interview subjects into saying things they might regret later. The Chief was smart enough to see what she could do to him if she pressed the wrong buttons. PR could be picking up the pieces for months."

"Why has she taken an interest in Ernie Noguera?" asked Jesse. "What's her special angle?"

"Her one and only interest is to keep people tuned to her channel," said Sandy. "And she's discovered that the best way to do that is to be controversial. So she keeps shouting out 'police whitewash' to anyone who will listen."

"All right then," said Jesse wearily. "I'll talk to her. Which parts of the investigation can I use to convince her differently?"

"The stuff you can use is all contained in this file that Altobelli had prepared," said Sandy, handing Jesse a plastic-coated sheaf of papers. As Jesse began to leaf through them Sandy picked up his newspaper. "Oh, and Jesse," she added mischievously, flicking back from the sports pages until she reached the fashion, "if you're going on TV maybe you should change your tie."

To Jesse's surprise, the interview at KBX studios went surprisingly smoothly. Rita Henderson asked him little about the investigation and instead concentrated on Ernie Noguera and his family. She seemed a patient and sympathetic listener and it was only later, back at the department, when he watched the KBX early evening news, that he realised how she had set him up – and as the realisation dawned, Jesse found himself growing angry and dismayed at the way that the attractive, red-headed reporter had managed it.

"On the one hand is the evidence against Officer Noguera," said Rita Henderson on the portable TV on Sandy's desk. "The banknotes with the matching serial numbers, the clown's mask and the gun that seven separate witnesses all testified were identical to the mask and the gun used in three of the robberies, and the maps and timetables of the security systems – all of these were discovered in Officer Noguera's garage. On the other hand, as Officer Mach pointed out, there is Ernest Noguera's exemplary service record. However, what Officer Mach did NOT point out is that he and the deceased had been close personal friends for a number of

years. Meanwhile, with more than two hundred thousand dollars unaccounted for, Ernest Noguera's widow will continue to receive a pension from the city at least until the investigation is closed. The question that must be asked is exactly how much evidence will the department need before they do finally consider the investigation closed? This has been Rita Hen . . ."

Jesse reached out and stabbed the set's off button, then picked up the phone and dialled KBX. "Doesn't she realise what a report like that could do to Carmen and the kids?" he asked Sandy angrily as he waited for a reply on the phone.

When the girl on the KBX switchboard answered, he asked her to put him through to Rita Henderson. The girl told him that Rita Henderson was unavailable as she was busy preparing for an interview she had that evening, then she asked Jesse if he'd care to leave a message.

"Just tell her that Officer Mach called," said Jesse irritably. "And pass on my sympathies to whoever the poor dumb jerk is who's been saddled with the job of answering her questions."

"I doubt the mayor will appreciate being referred to as a poor dumb jerk, Officer Mach," said the switchboard operator curtly. "Nevertheless, I shall pass on your message if I get the opportunity." Then she hung up.

Jesse looked at the silent receiver in surprise for a moment then got a fresh line out and dialled Carmen Noguera. He'd just finished apologising for any distress the afternoon's interview might have caused her when the duty officer put his head around the door and said that Altobelli wanted to see him. Jesse asked him if he knew why the commander wanted him and the duty officer replied that he thought it had something to do with the Ernie Noguera case.

"Yeah," Jesse muttered to himself as he got to his feet, "I figured as much."

However, to Jesse's surprise, the duty officer led him not to Altobelli's office but to the department's communication room. There, the burly police chief was standing in front of an illuminated map of the city in his shirt sleeves, a look of harassed concern on his face. In front of him, at the base of the map on which signal lights were flashing on and off, sat three uniformed officers all wearing headphones.

"I watched your interview, Mach," said Altobelli, his manner suggesting he had other, more important problems pressing him, "and I figure that I owe you an apology. You and Mrs Noguera. See it was me that leaked the news of the Noguera investigation to the media. I had to do it to protect Noguera's partner. The two of them were working undercover trying to flush out a group of urban terrorists. They fixed the brakes on Noguera's bike and framed him for their own robberies when they rumbled he was a cop. I had to go along with the frame to protect the other man we had working on the inside. Turns out not to have done him any good though. We got a call this afternoon and . . ."

"The Cobra's back again, sir," said one of the uniformed officers, and Altobelli turned away from Jesse and picked up a hand mike from the desk in front of the policeman.

"All right then, Mister Police Chief," said a taunting voice on one of the speakers. "This time you got 30 seconds to find me."

"Cobra," said Altobelli urgently into the mike, "let me speak to Officer Robinson. Give us some indication that he's still alive."

"Oh, he's still alive, all right," laughed the voice. "All bug eyed and sweating. Right now he can't talk to you, though. If he tries to, then the gun I got in his ear is likely to go off. Talk to you again later."

"He's gone again, Commander," said the uniformed cop, removing the headphones from his head. "He's somewhere in the Long Beach area. That's as close as we could get."

"Alert all units in the area. Let me

know next time he calls," said Altobelli, with the faintest trace of weariness in his voice. Then he turned back towards Jesse. But Jesse, realising that the department were going to need the help of Street Hawk, had already gone.

"This dude who calls himself The Cobra keeps calling the department on Robinson's wire," said Jesse as he donned the shiny black helmet and checked its functions. "He's out there on the street keeping one jump ahead of the department's traces."

"You want me to run his signals through our own computers?" asked Norman, his hands working the console keys as Jesse fired the ignition on the sleek, turbo-assisted attack motorcycle.

"Right," said Jesse through the intercom as he felt the power of the engine coil and uncoil as he gunned the throttle. "And patch his signals through to me while you're doing it. You figure you can do that?"

Norman Tuttle gave Jesse Mach a thumbs up sign from where he sat at the computer console. He punched a button, and outside, the painted world on the camouflaged hideout split in two as the doors slid back. Jesse Mach put the bike into forward drive and with man and machine so close as to seem as one, they leapt, roaring, from the command centre, skidded between pallets and crates, then hit the street at 80 mph. Winding the machine up to 150 mph once he was on the Long Beach Freeway, slotting through tiny gaps in the night time traffic, Jesse raced towards the area where the department had last picked up a signal from The Cobra. As soon as he had reached Willows, Jesse eased the bike down to 60, and took the ramp down to the surface road. He had just crossed the Willows Avenue and Norman told him to take the San Diego Freeway.

The neon and streetlights began to turn into a blur as they flashed across the gleaming visor. The speed signal in the corner went up to 100-plus as Jesse pulled out to overtake a cattle truck, tucked in again in front of the truck to avoid an oncoming coach, then gave the throttle a squirt to beat a red light. As the black motorcycle shot across the intersection, Norman patched The Cobra and Altobelli into Jesse's helmet.

"You get a little longer this time, Mister Detective Man," said The Cobra's cruel, mocking voice as Jesse sped up the ramp onto the freeway, where he opened the throttle and took the bike up to almost 200 mph. "See, I figure I'll make it easy for you guys to pick up the pieces of your boy once he's gone."

"Computer has him heading north on Harbour," interrupted Norman. "Can you make the turn?"

"Because this is your last call, Mister Altobelli," said The Cobra, as Jesse opened the air foils just enough to drag the speed down to a level that enabled him to make the turn onto the Harbour Freeway. "Once I'm through talking then I waste your man Raymondo. You got any messages for the officer before his head comes off?"

"Cobra." Jesse heard Altobelli's desperate voice almost pleading as

he brought the air foils back in, leaned the cycle over, then went past a line of traffic on the dirt shoulder before peeling away onto the Harbour Freeway filter. "Wasting Ray isn't going to do you any good."

"Wrong, Altobelli," chuckled The Cobra. "It ain't going to do HIM any good. We trusted him, see? Him and his buddy Ernie. They turned us, man, and now . . ."

"Target eight miles ahead," Norman interrupted. "Going to hyperthrust." He went through the countdown, and then the bike kicked beneath Jesse as it accelerated suddenly to 300 mph, and the sound of The Cobra's voice was lost in the sounds of the wind howling across the motorcycle's fairing. Solid objects seemed to disappear and the tail lights and headlights fused into a dizzying tunnel of diamond light as Jesse pressed down low across the tank and watched the target range figure in the top right corner of his visor gradually shrink. When it fell below a mile, Norman switched him back to manual controls and Jesse eased the bike down to 100.

"You should have it on visual now," said Norman. "You got anything?"

Jesse looked at the freeway up ahead. Three kids in a customised Buick were in the middle lane, and a tan Oldsmobile with a man smoking a cigar was cruising alongside them. Just ahead, on the inside lane, was a silver panel truck. Jesse switched to infra-red, pulled in behind it, and locked the particle beam gun onto attack mode.

"You got him," Jesse heard Norman say as he locked onto his target and loosed a wriggling, flashing, fizzing blue stream of laser particles at the van's back axle. The heat fused the cogs and bearings in the transmission system and the van slewed wildly across the road, crunched into the central barrier, then veered back across to the side banking, where it rolled over and came to a halt with its wheels spinning in the air. Jesse skidded to a halt, leapt from his bike and hauled a twisted rear door open only to find himself looking down the barrel of a Smith & Wesson. The gun was in the hands of a bleach-haired man. He seemed dazed and blood was running from a cut on his forehead down onto the lid of a single, narrow, calculating eye. The other was covered by an eyepatch.

"Just hold it right there, whoever you are," the man said, and Jesse recognised the voice as The Cobra's. "Put your hands up in the air and turn around."

As Jesse began to do as he had been ordered, he caught a slight movement from further back in the van and suddenly an arm reached out and forced The Cobra's gun hand up into the air. It fired twice, harmlessly, and the The Cobra's assailant forced the gun from his grasp and Jesse reached forward and grabbed it as it spun across the roof of the van beneath them.

"Thanks, mister," said the man who had disarmed The Cobra. "I don't know who you are, but you got here just in time. I'm a police officer and these guys were going to kill me. I've got to get to a phone, and quick. I've got to get through to my commanding officer, to tell him to put an extra guard out on the mayor. There's a squad of crazies planning to snatch him tonight. With half the police department trying to find out where I was they figured the security around him wouldn't be so tough. Maybe you could . . ." Officer Raymond Robinson's voice trailed off as he saw the black-clad figure of the ex-motorcycle cop turn away and sprint back to his gleaming black supercycle. In the distance the siren on an approaching black and white rang across the night.

With no time to wait for a gap in the traffic, Jesse cut in the air jets, jumped his motorcycle across the central crash barrier, and headed southward toward the studios of KBX TV.

As he came off the freeway at El Segundo then beat it through the streets toward the television station Norman's voice told him to back off and leave the mayor's kidnap to the police.

"You're forgetting, Norman," said Jesse, the bike seeming to pivot on his knee as he dropped the speed down and made an extraordinarily sharp right, "I *am* a cop."

As he pulled in at the front entrance to KBX Jesse could hear the sound of gunfire. A security guard lay wounded on the entrance steps and he told Jesse that three men had gone into the building. Jesse thanked him, called over a passing secretary to help see to the injured man's wounds, then asked which studio the mayor was in. The guard pointed to a first storey window above the entrance foyer and said that the mayor was waiting there until it was time for his interview to take place.

Jesse drove his bike back down the TV station's looping driveway and then turned toward the building and opened the throttle. As the distance between the bike and the brick wall shrank he fired the compressed air vertical lift jets, and the supercycle immediately took off, soared noisily over the foyer, and came smashing in through the plate glass window. Three hooded men stood in the doorway holding machine guns, and they looked up in alarm as the black bike burst into the room in front of them in a shower of flying fragments of glass. Jesse caught a glimpse of the mayor and Rita Henderson diving for safety beneath the table as he dropped the bike in a controlled skid and its still-spinning wheels slammed into the three attackers' legs at knee height, sending them flailing to the ground like animated skittles. He kicked a machine gun across the floor to where one of the mayor's bodyguards was lying face down with his hands over his head. Then he hauled the sleek black motorcycle upright and drove through the open doorway into the corridor.

Commander Altobelli arrived at the TV station just in time to see the streamlined shape of the million dollar motorcycle smash through the glass doors of the foyer, bounce down the steps, and streak past him at 120 mph.

He was still talking about the incident the following day when Jesse went in to see him.

"Yes, Mach," he asked impatiently, "what do you want?"

Jesse kept his face straight. "There's a group of reporters here who want to know whether the motorcycle rider who stopped the snatch on the mayor last night was attached to the department."

"You're the PR man," said the police chief. "Tell them the same thing the mayor told them – 'No comment'."

HAWK SQUARE

By reading up, down, diagonally, backwards and across, can you find the names of the following two wheelers in the Hawk Square?

BATAVUS
BENELLI
BETA
BMW
BSA
CAGIVA
CASAL
COSSACK
CZ
DUCATI
ENFIELD INDIA
FANTIC
GARELLI
GILERA
HARLEY DAVIDSON
HONDA
JAWA
KAWASAKI
LAMBRETTA
LAVERDA
MALAGUTI
MORINI
MOTOBECANE
MOTOGUZZI
MZ
SERVETA
STREET HAWK
SUZUKI
TRIUMPH
VESPA
YAMAHA

K	A	W	A	Z	U	K	I	H	A	W	K	S	T	R	E	E	L	X	P
A	Y	A	M	A	D	A	V	I	D	S	U	Z	U	T	T	A	L	L	I
Z	A	H	L	L	I	Z	Z	U	G	O	T	O	M	F	U	I	R	T	A
A	B	A	C	U	Z	Z	S	T	R	E	E	H	A	W	L	K	I	W	I
W	O	M	N	A	L	A	S	A	K	I	C	T	D	E	B	U	D	G	I
A	L	A	M	B	R	E	T	T	A	J	R	K	L	M	N	O	E	P	Q
K	A	Y	I	N	I	E	X	R	D	I	F	L	E	M	O	Z	N	O	R
I	V	S	T	R	V	E	E	T	U	A	P	S	E	V	H	O	F	A	W
W	E	S	T	R	E	E	K	M	N	T	W	A	H	B	S	O	I	D	K
A	R	K	E	L	I	G	P	T	I	S	A	C	U	D	I	N	E	M	E
I	D	S	W	M	B	H	I	R	L	E	Z	Y	I	D	A	V	L	I	N
K	A	W	S	A	K	C	A	S	S	O	C	V	H	N	O	S	D	D	A
A	W	A	U	K	H	H	A	W	S	M	A	L	A	G	U	T	I	K	C
S	U	Z	U	K	I	T	A	C	U	D	S	V	Z	V	P	I	N	O	E
A	U	Z	A	W	A	T	E	T	Y	K	A	W	A	D	I	S	D	N	B
W	H	V	A	W	T	A	G	E	U	B	L	B	A	R	E	L	I	G	O
A	S	G	A	R	E	L	L	I	R	E	B	U	G	A	T	T	A	K	T
K	Z	J	M	T	P	R	O	B	O	T	O	A	V	I	G	A	C	Z	O
W	A	S	A	W	A	K	I	S	B	A	S	B	S	I	N	I	R	O	M
A	D	N	O	H	X	B	E	N	E	L	L	I	T	E	R	B	M	A	L

THE MEAN ARENA

Inside the secret Street Hawk command centre, Norman Tuttle ran the grainy monochrome tape yet again and stopped at the precise moment the black-suited motorcyclist stepped off his gleaming black machine and fired a burst from a Beretta Model 12 9mm submachine gun into the ceiling of the bank.

"There," said Norman, pointing at the bike. "You can see where he's removed the box section aluminium swing arm. It's a Kawasaki all right. A KLR250, I think. A DOHC four-stroke, four valve single. Looks like he modified the fairings himself."

"It's a keen machine," nodded Jesse Mach, "but we're talking hyperthrust."

"We are, yes. But to someone looking down the barrel of a loaded gun, one black crash-helmet on a fast bike is very much like another."

"I still don't see why this affects us."

Norman ran more film. "He's knocked over four banks in the last week. He can handle that bike. Our men want the cops to nail him. Until that man's caught and exposed, we've got to cancel Operation Street Hawk."

Jesse slumped unhappily in his chair. "You can't compare a souped-up roadster with my sweetheart," he moaned.

Norman winced. "We both know what my machine is capable of, Jesse. But we've got public opinion to think of. I got word from the top: Street Hawk stays at home."

The next day, with news of the latest bank robbery splashed across the front pages of every newspaper in town, Jesse Mach stood up to face the press alone. The commander had claimed a meeting with the mayor, and Sandy was presenting the money raised by the police raffle to a local orphans' home.

As usual, Larry led the questioning. "Why do you think Street Hawk turned bad?" he asked.

"We have no evidence these crimes were committed by –"

"You think the Robin Hood stuff went to his head?" Larry interrupted. "I mean, three weeks ago he cleared all the muggers off the Strip, and now he's sticking up banks. This guy just won't go away – and still you cops can't finger him. Don't you think it's time you tried something new?"

"I, er . . ." Jesse didn't know what to say. He was still annoyed at Norman for going along with the Feds and giving up without a fight. He would have liked nothing better than to meet his impersonator on the streets face to face. Then everybody could see that when it came to motorcycles his all-terrain pursuit vehicle was the finest piece of engineering in the whole wide world. "I . . . er . . . I'm sure the commander will answer that personally at a later date." Jesse looked round uncomfortably, cursing the fact that Sandy wasn't by his side, helping to take some of the flak.

In fact, at that very moment, Sandy was taking flak of a very different kind, and it was unlikely Jesse would have wanted to be too close to her side. She'd been in the act of drawing the cheque for the orphans' home when the doors of the bank had burst open and a large black motorcycle had skidded in. When the rider fired a burst of automatic fire into the ceiling and ordered everybody to lie down, Sandy had made a dive for an alcove. She hadn't been quick enough and now, pressed against a cool marble wall, she was holding her head in her hands as a second burst peppered the wall inches from her head, stinging her cheeks with splinters and powdering her hair with a thin, grey dust. If Jesse had been next to her he'd have been a certain casualty, a stone cold victim of acute lead poisoning. When the shooting stopped Sandy imagined she could hear distant bells fighting to create a coherent tune above the awful roaring in her ears.

And then the sounds of the bells seemed to change, and as the roaring died away Sandy recognised them for what they were – police sirens, two of them, hurrying to the scene. The black-helmeted head swivelled sharply round, a leather-gloved fist turned the throttle, and as the glinting black machine circled for the door, the rider grabbed Sandy roughly by the arm, pulled her across his petrol tank, and knocked her senseless with an expert rabbit punch to the pressure points behind her left ear.

He opened the clutch and as the bike jumped the steps at the front of the bank, he riddled the lead black and white with 9mm fire, smashing in the front windscreen as the patrolmen dived out of the doors. The second squad car took it in the front off-tyre, swerved through a pavement artist's latest collection of self-portraits, scattered a chanting group of shaven headed men in long yellow robes, and, after skimming under the hastily lifted stilt of a man in a red and white top hat and matching trousers, slammed to a halt under four crates of fresh watermelons. Before the officers had opened the doors, rider and hostage had vanished.

Early that night, in the command

centre, Norman and Jesse were finding it hard to agree.

"Believe me, Jesse, I'm just as angry as you are – but the answer is still no!"

"'One million or she dies'," quoted Jesse, smacking his palm with his walking stick. His eyes focussed in the middle distance and the muscles on his cheek rose and fell as he gritted his teeth. "And then he had the nerve to tell them it was Street Hawk calling!"

"You've got to try and calm down, Jesse. We're still grounded."

"You know how much Altobelli's got on his plate? He can't spare enough men."

"The Bureau will do all –"

"Someone somewhere knows where Sandy's being held. The answer's out there, Norman – on the street!"

"I guess you're right, Jesse," Norman finally conceded. "Suit up. You can take her out tonight, but unless it's absolutely impossible to avoid direct action, you've got to promise me to stick to surveillance only."

Jesse grabbed his specially contoured riding suit. "I'll be keeping my eyes open."

Within half an hour, after checking out a false trail in the West Bay, Jesse was tooling along Wilmington, between Pacific and Anaheim, at a steady 60 mph, when the savage shriek of an emergency siren sounded up behind. Without even looking back he hung a left down Denni Street, opened her up, and left the squad car standing on his way to Alameda. The worried voice of his immediate superior sounded inside his helmet.

"They're setting up a road block at Fling," Norman warned.

"I can jump it."

"If the cops are chasing you, they won't be chasing whoever's got Sandy."

Jesse hit the brakes, cut outside a red pick-up and just made the turn into Avalon. A sudden surge of power and he was passing the Harbour Steam Plant on his way to John S. Gibson Boulevard. After passing a black and white in San Pedro he put together some serious high-speed bendswinging until he found himself by a tall fence shaded by palms. He cut out the engine and tuned in his acoustic sensors. On the other side of the fence, on the forecourt of a fast food restaurant, a group of shirtless men in sleeveless denim jackets stood around a variety of motorcycles. Loud laughter rang in the night air as they rubbished each other's machines, told jokes, drank beer and ate hamburgers, waiting for everyone to arrive so they could start their run.

"I tell you, Rats – the Low Rider is the finest thing on the road today."

"Snake – I have told you before. It may look pretty, but you sure feel a fool when you drop it. For distance you need the Electra Glide."

"I may like to Glide when I'm old and grey –"

"You're bald, Snake."

"And you're ugly, Rats. Your momma used to feed you with a catapult. I still say the Low Rider's got the edge on everything . . . excepting Street Hawk, of course."

"You don't believe that stuff, do you? Man, that's hogwash!"

"That ain't hogwash, my man. I've seen the dude. Yesterday. Up near Redondo. They say that hog of his can fly!"

Behind the fence, Jesse switched on the power and, using the perfect road-holding of the million dollar machine to cut through the streets to Western Avenue, asked Norman for a hyperthrust countdown.

"8 . . . 7 . . . 6 . . ."

Jesse counted off the numbers as the gleaming pursuit bike swung out into the traffic. Then Norman cut in the hyperthrust from his computer assist panel, the turbos roared, and the glistening piece of high-tech hardware reared up on its back wheel. They had travelled almost a mile before Jesse got the front wheel down, and then he hung on for all he was worth as the mighty machine cut through the traffic like an arrow through fog, whistling into and out of the narrowest of gaps on Norman's computer-assisted course. After Alta Vista Park had passed like a smudge of hurtling greenery, Norman cut out the hyperthrust and Jesse took over manual control. A few blocks ahead, Jesse could see an ominous red glow in the sky.

Jesse headed for the fire, his screeching supercycle twisting down side alleys until it came in sight. The building was an old, seemingly deserted, four-storey block of flats, and bright red flames licked upward from the ground floor windows. Jesse was looking for any sign of Sandy or the bank-robber cyclist when Norman's shrill voice snapped a warning.

"Jesse! Look out! There's a rope!"

Norman was too late. The rope, stretched across a narrow street alongside the blazing building, caught Jesse just below the throat, ripped his hands from the controls, jerked his legs into the air and, as his riderless machine skidded into a wall, flung him flat on his back with a force that seemed to knock every trace of breath from his body. Jesse rolled over on the floor, gasping, wondering whether he would live long enough to find out which of his bones were broken. At the end of the street, silhouetted by the blazing building, a tall figure in black stepped out of the shadows. In his hands he carried a Beretta Model 12.

"Your wings are clipped, Street Hawk." The mocking voice came from behind the black visor of a crash helmet. "This is one worm that turned. You ain't fit for budgie seed now."

Jesse heard Norman's voice urging him to stand up and fight as the figure walked slowly towards the fallen superbike. Jesse got up on one elbow as the figure bent down and slowly lifted the glinting black bike.

"It started as a bit of a joke,

Street Kiwi," he went on. "But now the joke's over. The bike's mine. And – before I forget – the cop lady's upstairs in that building – trussed up like a chicken. Oven ready!" His cold, mad laughter rose against the crackling flames as he swung his leg across the shiny black seat of the crime-fighting motorbike and aimed his Beretta straight at Jesse's head.

And then the turbo-designed marvel, failing to register his partner's computer signature, activated its defence mechanism, whipping the seat up and sending the bank robber somersaulting into a pile of garbage. Jesse was climbing slowly to his knees when a choked cry came from the blazing block and he looked up to see Sandy on a fourth floor ledge, holding her hankie to her mouth to try and counter the thick black smoke billowing out of the open window beside her. Jesse pushed himself to his feet, staggered across the street and climbed aboard his bike.

"You can't make the jump," Norman cautioned. "It's too high!"

"Who mentioned jumping?" Jesse gunned the motor and his power-assisted partner crashed through the blazing front door, brushed aside a fallen, blackened beam and raced up the burning stairs. Between the second and third floors his luck ran out and as the stairs collapsed in a flurry of flame and sparks he cut in the compressed air jets, soared out of the torrent of fire, and, after a few heart stopping seconds when it seemed the spinning wheels could get no purchase on the smouldering plants and beams, surged up the last flight of stairs.

"You'd better get out quick, Jesse. You're overheating!"

Jesse ignored Norman's warning and called out for Sandy. She staggered in through the window clutching her throat and Jesse swung her over the saddle behind him.

"Hold tight!"

Jesse turned the throttle, let out the clutch and aimed the bike for the window.

On the ground the bystanders, drawn by the sight of the flames, uttered a collective gasp of astonishment when from out of the poisonous, rolling clouds of smoke, a jet black motorcycle came speeding into the night skies. It seemed briefly, as the two-wheeled steed sailed across the starry backdrop, that the futuristic motorcycle could actually fly, but then the early momentum of Jesse's daring gamble ran out, and the bike began dropping, its speed remorselessly increasing as the ground rose up to meet it. A woman screamed and Jesse hit the compressed air jets again ten feet from the street. The boosters hissed angrily and the expected deadly impact was dispersed in steam and dust as the vertical lift system's compressed air jets slowed the frightful plunge, and after two bone-jarring bounces that took the off-road hydraulic suspension system to its limits, Jesse's know-how, daring and skill saved the day. He brought the bike to a stop and, the tension gone, the stunned crowd burst out in a spontaneous bout of cheering, laughing and clapping.

Jesse turned to Sandy. "You OK?" he asked. Sandy nodded. While Jesse was helping her gently off the bike, he heard the yowling sound of racing engines and a black shape zipped across the opening at the end of the street. Jesse wrenched the throttle and set off in pursuit.

"Leave it to the cops, Jesse," urged Norman as he watched the road spinning under the bike's cameras. "They've got the place sealed up tight. There's nowhere for that nut to go!"

"Sorry, Norman." Jesse upped the revs. "This freak need his flakes shaking off."

Inside a nearby football stadium, a floodlit coaching session was coming to an end. The coach was wrapping up an experimental defensive play for the next big game when the first of the black motorcycles burst out of the players' tunnel, skidded across the plastic turf, swerved and stopped, its black-clad rider standing astride the steaming machine with his arm outstretched and a Beretta Model 12 trained on the tunnel.

"That's Street Hawk!" said a defensive tackle.

"You sure?" asked the quarterback.

"Sure I'm sure – that cat's bad!"

A thin humming sound from the tunnel grew suddenly louder, and when the first motorcyclist began emptying the 40 round magazine of his Model 12, players, coaches, officials and hangers-on all ran for the safety of the stands. As the red hot slugs bounced round the tunnel entrance the humming developed into a full-bodied, lung-searing howl of strength, and Jesse burst from the tunnel on his power-packed partner, re-engaging the compressed air vertical lift system while he weaved an evasive course.

The big black bike soared over the bank-robber, landed cleanly, and turned. Although his opponent was busily trying to reload, Jesse forsook his particle beam gun. One soft rubber bullet disarmed his evil doppelgänger and from then on Jesse was happy to lead the gun-crazy thief a merry dance along the dirt track, up and down the rows of seating, and around and around the plastic pitch.

He finally called time out by luring the desperate kidnapper onto his tail and breaking down the centre of the field. He slowed the revs enough for his pursuer to come in close as he homed in on the supporting stanchion of the goals and then, when it seemed impossible that he could avoid the solitary white pole, he opened his air foils to maximum and stabbed at the vertical jets. As if flicked by a giant finger, the high horsepower hyperthrust rose straight up in the air, and in the full glare of the floodlights, slowly completed a backward flip, landing heavily on the pitch in time to see his enemy's rushing machine slam head-on into the supporting pole. The pole creaked and rocked, the bike spun round and round in a small circle, and the black helmeted villain flew through the air, bounced, then rolled and skidded right out of the end zone. Jesse checked he was still alive and then, as he steered his super-sophisticated partner back out of the tunnel, the quarterback turned to his defensive tackle.

"I think you got it wrong, buddy," he smiled. "That cat's so bad he's good. THAT'S STREET HAWK!"

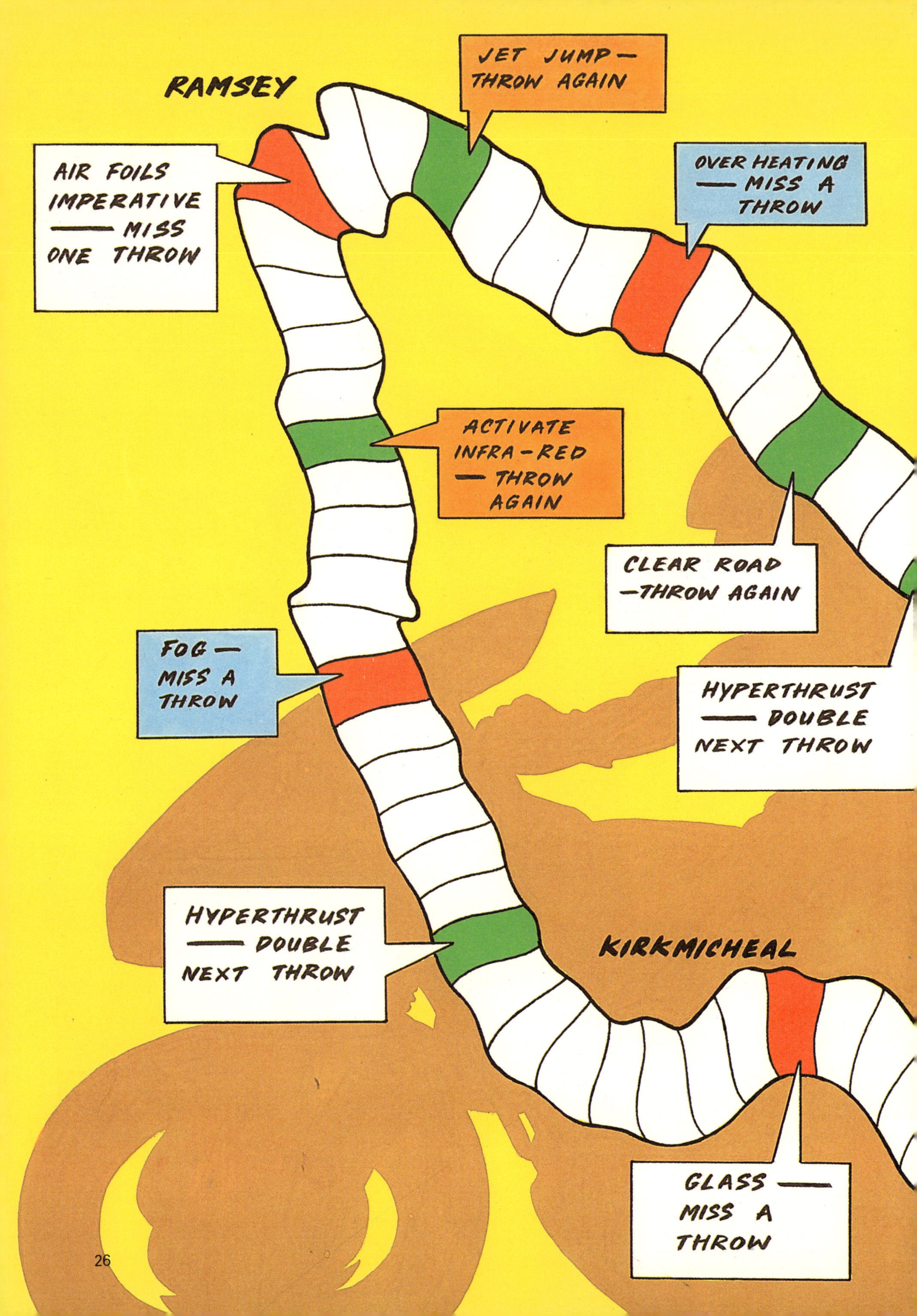
RAMSEY
JET JUMP— THROW AGAIN
AIR FOILS IMPERATIVE —— MISS ONE THROW
OVER HEATING —— MISS A THROW
ACTIVATE INFRA-RED — THROW AGAIN
CLEAR ROAD —THROW AGAIN
FOG— MISS A THROW
HYPERTHRUST —— DOUBLE NEXT THROW
HYPERTHRUST —— DOUBLE NEXT THROW
KIRKMICHEAL
GLASS —— MISS A THROW

STREET HAWK!

The Isle of Man TT races are among the most exciting – and dangerous – in the world. That's why, when researching the demands that would be put on both his supercycle and its rider, Norman Tuttle rigged up a computer mock-up of the entire 37¾ mile mountain circuit – then threw in some added hazards as well. Jesse and the bike passed with flying colours, but could you? Find out by playing this game.

A game for two or more players.
Players must begin on the START space and move towards Quarter Bridge.
If players land on a space containing instructions they must obey them.
If a player throws a six he may throw again.
If two players land on the same space they both miss a throw.
The winner is the first player back to the start.

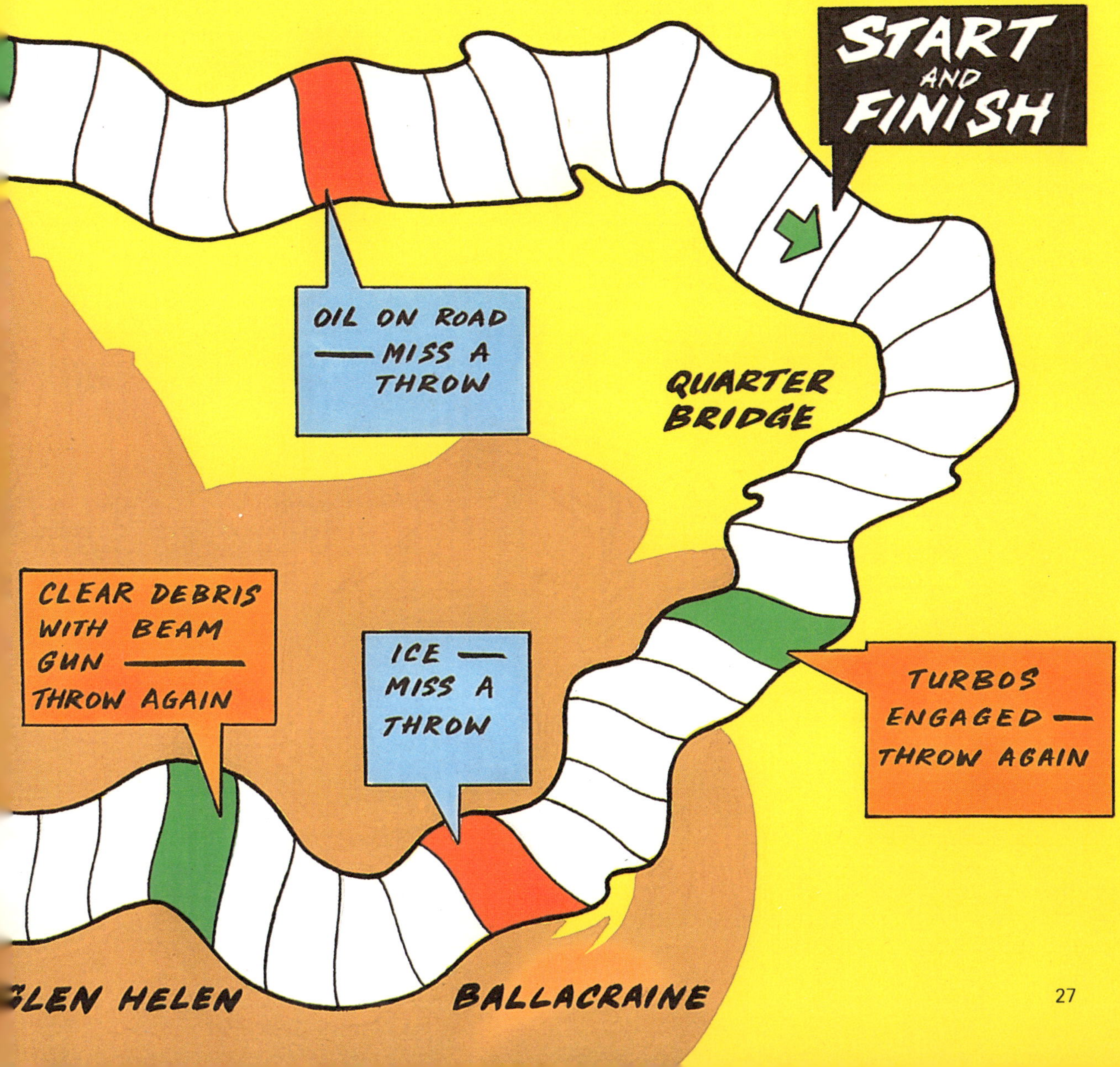

THE BITERS BIT

Venice, California: 2.38pm. The fresh sea breezes mingle with the bizarre aromatic cocktail of coconut suntan lotion, frying onions, burning rubber and cordite. For once, the Beach Park's carefree amateur circus of freaks, acrobats, weightlifters, clowns and jugglers has packed up its psychological tent and closed down the show. Elaborate picnics lie uneaten on the sand. A hot dog stall stands unattended, steaming in the sun. The cop in the black running shorts and LAPD T-shirt has taken off his roller skates and is leaning into a black and white, pitching his way to another box of ammunition for the police issue revolver in his conspicuous holster. The dance-crazy roller skating regulars have abandoned their specially marked paths, and although all their radios are still tuned to the same station, it's no longer the pulsating, uplifting raunch of Prince blasting out. The sound they all strain to hear is the sobering, careful, laconic delivery of a local radio reporter, fingered by fate to dance the swaying tightrope of drama unique to on-the-spot coverage of potentially bloody catastrophe. Venice, the prime fishing hole for the ten-second screwball spots tacked onto the regular bulletins, the whacky release valve for a nation building up steam – today Venice, mainstream America's favourite crazy cousin, has become headline news all on its own. Rock hard, white hot news. As the colourful inhabitants press against the police cordon and the firemen stare impotently at the blazing, upturned squad car, a young man with a mischievous smile and an unnerving glint in his pale blue eyes sits cross-legged on the roof of a crowded yellow school bus and rests his hand lightly on the T-shaped plunger of an old fashioned box detonator. A thin green wire runs from the box to the four large packs of gelignite strapped to his chest. The selfish squawking of seagulls, squabbling over crusts, blows in from the sea.

Commander Altobelli puts the megaphone to his mouth and talks as soothingly as his anger, frustration, and general animosity will allow. The man smiles. On the roofs of the muralled houses behind him, police marksmen take up their positions. Out of sight of the bus, behind a commandeered delivery truck, a SWAT team gets ready for action. Two men in grey suits, their appearance grave, talk quietly by the commander's car. A small man with a woollen hat puts down the cart full of paintings he is pushing and drifts to the back of the crowd.

And then a passing car backfires, a woman screams, the crippled squad car's fuel tank ignites with a cacophonous whirlwind of noise, and an undulating, rolling column of fire mushrooms uselessly into the air. Sudden, expectant gut-churning fear grabs the participants, passing through the crowd like an electric current, stretching time to the edge of hysteria, squeezing the senses to bursting point, paralysing nerves, brightening colours, sharpening sounds – putting action on hold as each panic-charged second takes on the passing speed of the single white liner on the horizon behind.

Then the man's hand starts slowly downward and the breaking spell is smithereened by the bellowing, wrathful howl of tormented power, as hypercharged motorcycle engines strain to the limit to reach the scene in time. The man's hand wavers, there is the sudden, violent hiss of activating air jets, and he looks up to see a pitch black figure astride a polished black supercycle, streaking through the air towards him, both man and machine glinting ominously in the bright afternoon sun.

The man smiles again, there is the sharp THWUP! of a single, soft-rubber round being fired, and he slams the plunger down into the box. Terrified screams freeze mid-throat strangled with hope, as the expected carnage fails to erupt. The man lifts the plunger and drives it down again, then again – his face afire with a savage, pained, bewildered fury. The men in the grey suits, seeing that the perfectly-aimed rubber bullet has ripped the wire from the box, spring on the top of the bus, kick away box and wire, hurl the man flat on his face, and while one kneels on his neck and presses a gun to the crown of his head, the other roughly handcuffs his wrists behind his back.

The relief is so total that several minutes pass before anyone in uniform takes note of the freckle-faced boy pointing out that the man on the motorbike is nowhere to be seen. A female body builder, her skin glistening with oil, turns away from the scene and runs through a series of spectacular poses. "That's Street Hawk for you," she says, to no-one in particular. "When he's through, he sure don't hang around for no medals." A passing hip-hop dancer nods and retunes his radio. The cop puts his skates back on. Southern California slips back in the groove.

"I wouldn't like to go through it every day," said Norman Tuttle, after he and Jesse had run through the afternoon's events. "How come Altobelli gave you time off?"

"He didn't," smiled Jesse, tossing an empty paper cup up and down in his hand as his engineer partner slouched in his chair with his back to the console. "One of Senator Jones' advance party had cornered him about having his car stolen. Seems there were a lot of important documents in it. I was passing, and the commander dumped him on me. And when I heard about the kook on the bus, I bounced him onto Sandy – gave her the chance to explain why nobody's come up with a single lead in the latest rash of –"

"It's not a rash any more, Jesse – it's an epidemic! This ring's hotter than a fire in a pepper mill. And all good cars too. They're really organised. Haven't you heard anything on the street?"

Jesse shrugged. "Couple of whispers, nothing solid. Have you thought about my plan?"

"Planting a few choice cars and fitting them with directional finders?" Norman refreshed his own memory. "I got the bugs all right, but the Bureau wasn't too keen to lend us the cars. Entrapment and all that." Behind Norman's head, on the electronic map of the city, a winking yellow light began moving through the criss-cross pattern of streets.

Jesse caught the cup and crushed it. "Where exactly are these bugs, Norm?" he asked.

Norman turned defensively back to the console. "It's no good, Jesse," he insisted. "The Bureau says it's out of our . . ." His voice trailed off when he noticed the moving light for the first time. As he watched, a gleam of understanding flared into hot, indignant rage. "My car!" he fumed. "The bugs were in my car! And now those punks have stolen it!"

"Take it easy," grinned Jesse, tossing the crumpled cup into a bin and reaching for his helmet. "This could be just the break we're looking for."

Within a minute, the stray tom-cat rooting through the garbage sacks outside the secret Street Hawk command centre was scrabbling for the protection of an upturned packing case as the sound of booming motors swelled, the camouflaged doors slid open, and Jesse and his polished, potent, precision-built partner catapulted out of their lair, arching over the watching feline's fragile retreat before clunking heavily down and blasting away down the street. The echo of the thundering engines had long since faded when the cat finally emerged.

"Not too fast!" warned Norman over the communicator. "You don't want to panic them into making a run for it. They might crash my car."

"Don't worry about it, Norm," said Jesse, easing off the throttle. "You keep telling me where the car is and I'll stay one corner behind."

Jesse held back as Norman relayed the erratic course his stolen car was taking. Whoever had committed the theft certainly wasn't taking any chances on being followed. Jesse had crossed the LA River three times before Norman's car finally hit the Redondo Beach Freeway, heading out of town. Twenty minutes later it swung off Redondo, and after another ten minutes driving through pleasant, tree-lined suburbs, it pulled up opposite an amusement park and two men climbed out.

Jesse watched them walk casually over towards the park, then cruised into a thicket across the road and dismounted. "You stay here," he whispered, winking into the lens of his coal-coloured companion.

Back at the console, Norman gritted his teeth.

Jesse skirted the amusement park on foot, sticking to the shadows and keeping the two car thieves in sight. He watched them trying their luck on an air rifle range, and when the striped-shirted proprietor handed them something small that he couldn't make out, he followed them over to the Ghost Train.

Despite the growing lateness of the hour, the park was still crowded. Loud rock and roll music blared from the sound systems of the different rides, all but drowning the clatter of machinery and the laughter-filled screams of the riders. Barkers snapped their braces and waved their hats as they touted, full volume, for business. A gang of teenage boys by the Cyclone combed their hair and jokingly pushed each other around, making great play of ignoring the gang of teenage girls by the Roller Coaster. The girls, singing along to the records, laughing, chewing gum and dancing, made equal play of ignoring the boys. Small children with their mothers' skirts in one hand and helium-filled balloons in the other looked up and around in mute wonder. Icecream, popcorn, and hot-dog sellers loudly advertised their wares. Young park employees moved among the customers with studied athletic

cool, collecting fares and smiling at the girls. A man with an electric blue suit sat on the steps to the Roundabout, fanning his face with a bright red hat. Jesse noticed that when the two men made their way from the Ghost Train to the River of Fear he put on his hat and joined them.

Jesse stood inside a slot machine arcade as the three men climbed into the same boat on the River of Fear, and gently drifted down the channel into a tunnel. He was about to follow when he saw the hawk-faced man in the ticket kiosk suddenly produce a CLOSED sign and put it in the window. He waited, checked that the flat-bottomed fibreglass boats were still floating along the man-made currents, then crept round the back of the kiosk, slipped over the railing, jumped stealthily into a passing boat, and lay down.

As the sound of the pounding music receded along with the smell of candy-floss and diesel, Jesse stared up at the luminous bats, skeletons and monsters painted on the tunnel roof, and listened. He couldn't hear the three men ahead. The only sounds he could make out – besides the distant merriment of the park – were the lapping of the water, the faint hum of the paddles that moved the water along the channels, and – he closed his eyes and concentrated. Whatever the other sound was, it seemed to be coming from below and to the side. He raised his head, peered over the side of the boat, then climbed onto the wooden shore, where a wax model of Dracula stood in an upright coffin, clutching the papier-mâche stake in his heart. Another upright coffin beside the effigy had its lid shut.

Jesse pulled tentatively at the lid of the second coffin and was surprised to find it opened easily. He pushed at the coffin's back and it swung away from him, opening out into a narrow, unlit passage. He closed the lid behind him and went through.

The sound was louder now and Jesse picked out the familiar ring of metal striking metal, of blow torches, chains, hammers and dropped spanners. He followed the sound down the passage, through several openings and doors, until he found himself standing on a cramped metal platform with another passage behind him and a flight of metal steps, blocked off by a thick black curtain, ahead. He pulled the edge of the curtain to one side and a smile grew wide behind the reflective blackness of his helmet. Below him, in what once must have been an underground car park, small teams of men were working furiously on a fleet of expensive cars, switching plates and tyres, lifting out engines, respraying bodywork, tightening bolts, hammering out dents, fixing new doors and filing down chassis numbers in a text book display of a disciplined hot car ring in rapid efficient action.

Across the busy, noisy room, at the bottom of a ramp leading up to a wide metal door, Jesse saw the men he'd been tailing, holding out their hands and remonstrating with a long-haired, well-muscled man in a boiler suit. Jesse recognised him as Joe Flack, an ex-football star

gone bad. He had just let the curtain fall back when he felt the gun pressing against his spine.

"This is an automatic, buddy, so if you don't want a string of lead studs in your backbone, put your –"

Jesse dived forward and kicked up his heels. His computer-designed riding boots knocked the gun in the air, and as a prolonged burst of automatic fire ripped through the curtain, he tumbled underneath it down the sharp metal steps. He had time to see a snarling Joe Flack pull out the .357 Magnum from his overalls before a stray bullet sliced the main power cable and the underground workshop was plunged into almost total darkness.

Jesse took advantage of the night vision facility in his helmet by vaulting the remaining steps and slamming down the open bonnet of a Mercedes on the hand of the thug who'd been working on it. He jammed a tyre over the head of a scrawny guy with a paint gun, and the last thing he saw before he sneaked under the door at the top of the ramp was Flack, torch in hand, stuffing papers and money from a wall safe into a sack.

Flack had been ready for this moment for a long time, keeping the high denomination bills alongside all the documents and letters he'd collected with blackmail in mind. He bared his teeth in determination as he filled the sack. The time had come, and ever since High School he'd known just when to move. He'd never been so cool that he couldn't leave town. He moved. He planned . . .

But there was no way of planning for the black and white parked across his escape route, nor for the two plain clothes men who spotted him ducking back into the park, and when he hurdled the roller coaster turnstile and dived on the last car pulling out, he knew he had to think again, and think again fast. He hunkered down in the seat and hid, hugging his bag full of loot as the car rattled its way up the long slow haul to the top of the wooden hill. Then, when the car neared the crest and he chanced a quick look out, the blood in his veins seemed to freeze. With the cold silver rays of the moon streaming down to highlight their menacing contours, a man and a motorcycle straddled the track at the highest point of the ride, with the slight juddering of the exhaust the only movement to be seen. The man's impenetrable helmet was turned towards him and it seemed to Flack, as the car left the sounds of laughter and excitement further and further below, that both man and machine were waiting . . . waiting for him . . . and for justice.

Jesse gunned the throttle and his power-packed partner rose up almost vertically on its back wheel on the wooden slats by the side of the track. The car went by, the bike swivelled round, and as Flack began the white-knuckled plunge on the other side of the hill, Jesse went after him. Whatever cool Flack had once had completely deserted him during the rushing, clangorous fall. He dropped his gun on the floor of the car and when Jesse pulled alongside, he lashed out with his bag. Jesse grabbed it and as they raced even faster, a bundle of notes worked loose and fluttered down towards the excited crowd below. Seeing the large group of cops gathering at the end of the ride, Jesse wrenched the bag from Flack's grasp, cut in the air jets, zoomed past a startled couple on the Cyclone, then crashed through some bushes, skidded under a stationary trailer and turned up the throttle as he righted the bike on the open road. Within seconds, the uproarious snarling of his engines was lost in the night.

The following morning, having earlier assured the man from Senator Jones' camp that yes, his car had been recovered and no, there were no details of any documents and yes again, the Senator's visit to the orphanage would still go ahead, Jesse was enjoying a quick cup of coffee when Norman came through on the phone.

"Get over here quick!" Norman ordered. "I've just been through those papers you brought back last night. No wonder that guy wanted his car back. He's not who he says he is at all. His name is Kirk and he's leading a three-man team to assassinate the Senator."

Jesse almost knocked Sandy over in his haste to get to the command centre and by the time he was suited up and on the road, there were only three minutes left before the Senator was due at the orphanage. Then Norman engaged hyperthrust, turbos screamed, and Jesse hung on while his majestic metal motorcycle partner took him through the dazzling vortex of sight, sound and blistering speed. Norman cut out hyperthrust 100 yards from the orphanage and the air foils whined as they dragged the hurtling cycle to a halt in front of the Senator's car. Already, the windows of a black sedan across the road were slowly coming down and two lethal looking barrels were nosing out. Jesse flipped the beam gun onto stun and the dancing blue energy bolts leaped forward in a shimmering cerulean manifestation of power. The crackling rays sparked around the car until the bonnet flipped up, the headlamps exploded, and as the thin wisps of grey smoke began rising from the engine, the men inside slumped unconscious in their seats.

"Look out, Street Hawk!" cried a little girl. "Up there!" She pointed to a first floor window where a man in a ski-mask was looking down the sights of a high-powered rifle. Jesse roared forward, stood the bike up on its back wheel and let go the rubber slug. It caught the sniper on the shoulder and he whirled round inside the room before falling backwards out of the window and landing in a flower bed. Jesse went over and pulled off his mask. "Where's Kirk?" he demanded.

The man groaned. The sound of sirens grew closer. "C-Cabrillo Beach," he gasped. "Boat . . . got . . . got . . ." Suddenly the man's voice tailed off and his head slumped unconscious to one side. Jesse laid him down and climbed back on his bike and seconds later Norman had re-engaged hyperthrust. Jesse rode with it all the way to the harbour, his knees tucked in and his head down to reduce drag as the high-tech holocaust of furious sound and motion shot down a tunnel of light like a bullet down the barrel of a gun. Then Norman disengaged, and Jesse was taking her down when he spotted Kirk jumping into a cabin cruiser at the end of the fishermen's pier. He opened throttle, jet-jumped the barrier, and poured on the speed as he scorched past the rows of astonished anglers. Already Kirk was nearly 20 yards out to sea.

"Don't try it, Jesse," Norman pleaded. "You've insufficient velocity and –"

"And?" echoed Jesse, still accelerating when he came to the end of the pier. At the last moment he flipped on the jump jets and his potent pursuit vehicle soared into the air like a winged horse. Kirk turned and looked round for a gun but it was too late. As Jesse and his Pegasus-like partner dropped down from the sky he raised his hands in self defence, then wisely thought better of it and dived over the side. Man and machine clattered down on the well deck and careered through the open cabin door, finally pulling up only inches from a glass covered case filled with fishing rods. Jesse backed the bike out and stood it on the well deck. Kirk was floundering back towards the pier where Jesse could see the familiar figure of Altobelli gesticulating angrily. On the communicator, Norman's voice was warning him that if he ever did anything as foolhardy again he'd be dropped from the operation. Jesse looked up at the blue sky and thought of the fishing rods. If Kirk had been planning on a long trip there would probably be food and drink aboard as well. Altobelli was still angrily waving his arms. Norman was clucking like a mother hen. Jesse patted the gleaming fairings of his highly polished partner, fetched himself a can of Coke from the fridge inside, took the wheel, and headed out to sea. They could spare him for one afternoon. After all – his partner had never been fishing before.

THE NIGHT OF THE HAWK
A press conference following the seizure of a massive shipment of narcotics from South America . . .
POLICE
Commander Altobelli, do you think you've finally stamped out the drug menace?
I'd *like* to think so . . .
. . . but I don't. The problems are appalling. We just have to keep working away, hitting them when we can . . .
Not everyone is there to ask questions . . .
You won't be hitting anyone any more, creep!
. . . a small blow pipe . . .
SSSS
THWCK
. . . a poisoned dart . . .
. . . and the commander falls senseless.
ARGGH!
OOOH!
GASP!
Commander! What's wrong?
There he goes! Grab him!

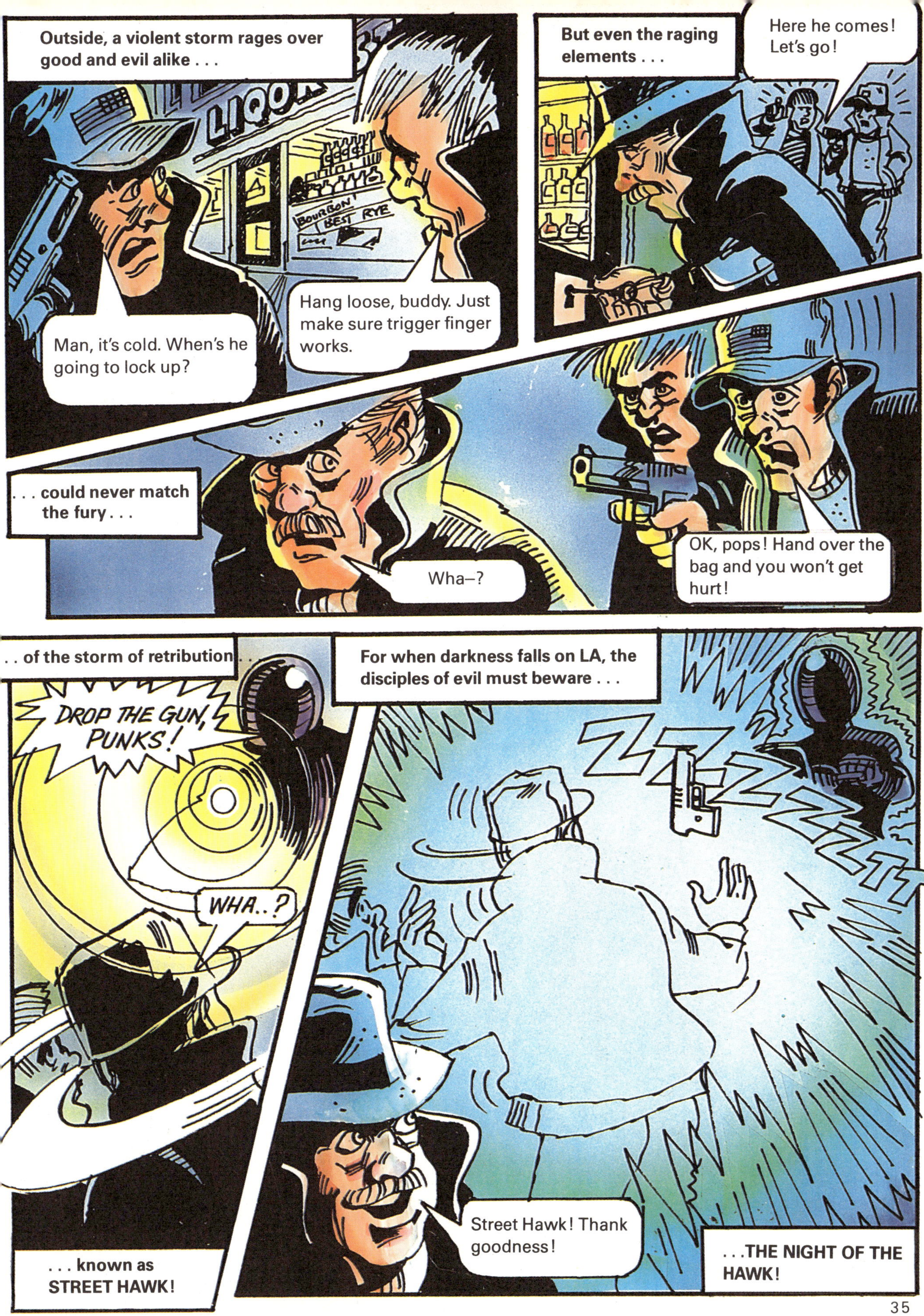
Outside, a violent storm rages over good and evil alike . . .
LIQUOR
BOURBON
BEST RYE
Man, it's cold. When's he going to lock up?
Hang loose, buddy. Just make sure trigger finger works.
But even the raging elements . . .
Here he comes! Let's go!
. . . could never match the fury . . .
Wha–?
OK, pops! Hand over the bag and you won't get hurt!
. . of the storm of retribution . . .
DROP THE GUN, PUNKS!
WHA..?
. . . known as STREET HAWK!
For when darkness falls on LA, the disciples of evil must beware . . .
Street Hawk! Thank goodness!
. . .THE NIGHT OF THE HAWK!

As the sound of a siren draws close. . .
You'd better stay here and tell them what happened.
But . . . but . . .
WHEEEEEOOOO
. . . Jesse cuts in the air jets . . .
. . . and LEAPS towards his next assignment!
HISSS
WHOOSSHH
Look out! We're going to –
. . . crash?
Uh? Where'd he go?
From inside the secret STREET HAWK command centre, Norman Tuttle relays the bad news.
The gang got their revenge, Jesse. Altobelli's been poisoned!
Is he dead?
No, but he's very ill – they think it's curare!
CURARE – a deadly poison isolated from *Chondrodendron tomentosum*. Though harmless when eaten, once injected into the bloodstream it eventually causes death through respiratory failure.
Is there anything I can do?
No way. The doctor's having some PROSTIGMIN flown in by helicopter.
PROSTIGMIN – instantaneously reverses symptoms of CURARE poisoning.
But, as Norman speaks . . .
KERRAAK
We're hit!

Mayday! Mayday! I can't hold her! We're going down!
KERUMP!
Norman intercepts the distress signal . . .
It's not too far away, Jesse. You could soon be there!
I'm on my way! Engage hyperthrust!
Hyperthrust achieved!
WHOOOSSHH!

Within half an hour . . .
You OK?
Sure. And the serum's intact – you'd better take it.
VRRM
Good luck!
VRROOM
But, as Jesse heads for the hospital . . .
Jesse – you'll have to turn back! The bridge at Cougar Canyon's down!
I can't! Once you're off the ground you'll be an unguided missile!
Just give me all you've got – and cut out when I yell!
It's too late now – I'll have to jump it.
Jesse – you can't! The bike won't take it!
We've got to go for it, Norm – give me hyperthrust!
NOW!
Hyperthrust discontinued. You're on manual!
WHOOOSSH!

SSSHHH!
A heavy landing . . .
THWUMP!
. . . a heart-stopping battle for control . . .
. . . and Jesse is home free!
You did it, Jesse
– brilliant!
Save it until you see what I've done to the suspension!
VRROOOOOM
Later, at the hospital . . .
You bust the drug ring, they grabbed the guy who tried to kill you – what are you looking so angry about?
I was just thinking – if Mach had been there doing his job – he might have been hit instead of me!
Thanks a million, chief!
M ALTOBELLI

THE MAN IN THE WHITE SUIT

Spansky flipped the safety catch on his snub-nosed automatic, touched briefly on the length of lead piping in his belt, then turned his leather collar up against the cold, sharp wind. A bitter smile flitted across his boyish face but his ageless, hunted eyes showed no pleasure. Go west, young man, they'd said. Go west to the land of opportunity. He'd already been north – and south – and since he'd started his trek in a 42nd Street jeweller's shop with a smoking gun in his hand, 85 dollars in his back pocket and a man lying bleeding on the counter – well, maybe they were right after all. Here he was at last in the Sunshine State, back up onto the coast with nowhere left to run between the Pacific breakers and a 30-year stretch in any one of eight different jails from Texas to Alaska. He looked anxiously at his watch. Two minutes. This was one score he needed so badly he could taste it. One big score to turn his luck around and put him on his feet again.

He ducked back into the shadows as a white car pulled up in front of the apartment building. Spansky held back while an old grey-haired man wearing a white flared suit and built-up brogues climbed out and began locking the door. Spansky felt his hearbeat quicken when he saw the brown leather attaché case in the man's hand. He drew the pipe from his belt and stepped forward.

The man turned before Spansky reached him. His eyes seemed bright with fear. "You want the case?" he asked, his voice shrill. "Take it!" He threw the case on the car boot. "Just don't hurt me, that's all! Leave me alone!"

With the gun in one hand and the lead pipe in the other, Spansky hesitated as the man backed away. The case was already close enough for him to grab. On the other hand, the old boy had got a good look at his face, and it wouldn't take long to . . .

Suddenly, the whistling of the wind and the myriad muted sounds of the city at night were drowned by the deafening growl of hyper-powered engines and the high-pitched squealing of rubber on road. Spansky turned and was immediately blinded by the intense beam of light that seemed to burn into the back of his skull. "What the –?" He held his gun hand up to his eyes. Squinting into the beam he could just make out a motionless figure, all in black, sitting astride a mean-looking motorbike of a design he'd never seen before. He hurled the lead pipe at the source of the beam and opened up with his gun at the rider. His gun jammed on the fourth shot. The figure in black never moved.

"Drop it, punk!"

Spansky ignored the order, desperately trying to free the spent slug stuck in the breech. On the bike, two stubby particle accelerator laser beam gun barrels swivelled into action. Inside the gleaming black helmet, Jesse Mach locked on his target, set for stun, and fired.

Spansky didn't know what had hit him. Suddenly the gun felt hot in his hands. Flashes of what looked like blue lightning were jumping all over him. The blood in his veins felt like boiling acid. He threw down his gun, staggered seven halting steps from the white car, then fell on his face in the gutter. Jesse switched off the beam gun, killed the light, and was climbing off his glistening machine when the case on the back of the car exploded.

The blast knocked Jesse backwards across the road. As he skidded and rolled he caught fleeting glimpses of flashing yellow flames and flying debris. When he finally got to his feet the car was engulfed in fire and the crackling flames, whipped by the wind, danced crazily upward into the night. Jesse looked up and down the road. Spansky was still in the gutter, shaking his head groggily, trying unsuccessfully to push himself up. There was no sign of the man in the white suit. Jesse remounted his mechanical partner, waited silently across the street until a black and white came and took Spansky away, then gunned his supercharged engine and headed back to command centre.

The following morning, in his other, low-profile role as an officer in the police department's public relations unit, Jesse was being briefed in what to say by a clearly irritated Commander Altobelli.

"Just don't mention Street Hawk, that's all," the commander snarled.

"You know they're going to ask, sir." Sandy tried to calm him down. "They've already dug up a witness who said he saw a flying motorcycle with a ray gun and a flamethrower."

The commander groaned. "Can't you just tell them – er . . . er . . . ah . . . um . . . tell them to get off my back and leave me alone to do my job in peace!" He thumped the desk with his fist so hard the cup of cold coffee wobbled, revealing a ring of sediment close to the rim.

"What about the guy we pulled in?" asked Jesse. "Has he been charged?"

"He will be," said Altobelli firmly, glad to be back on familiar territory. With punks you knew where you were. With crazy vigilantes on magic motorcycles . . .

"What with?" Jesse pressed.

The commander picked up the coffee, sipped and winced. "We can hold him on a weapons charge for now. We've already had wires from all over the country. The creep's wanted in eight states."

"What's his story?" asked Sandy.

Commander Altobelli rolled his eyes. "That he was on his way to buy a milkshake."

"Any address?" Jesse asked, notebook in hand.

"It's on the file."

"Anything on the car?"

Altobelli looked at Jesse like a bulldog at a poodle. "You're PR, Mach – not detective. Now get out there and do your job. Which – in case you've forgotten – means keeping those nosey muckrakers out of police affairs!"

Sandy's eyes grew hard. "I think there's a little more to it than that, Commander," she began icily.

Altobelli didn't hear her. He'd already picked up his jacket from the back of his chair and was striding purposefully for the door.

After the hectic press conference, when he'd had to answer questions ranging from the police attitude towards UFOs to the possibility of secret death squads, Jesse finally caught up with the officer in charge of the Spansky case. It seemed that since Altobelli had seen the file, Spansky, confronted with a mountain of evidence from his villainous past, had broken down and spilled. He claimed he'd been collared by a man in a bar who'd told him about his sister's new boyfriend – how he was rolling in money, how he drove a brand new car, how he always picked her up at exactly the same time three nights a week.

"You get anything on the car?" Jesse asked.

The officer nodded as he showed Jesse the door. "Sure – it was stolen from the airport three weeks ago."

That night, Jesse and Norman ran what they'd got through the computers in the command centre.

"What was in the case?" asked Jesse as Norman's practised fingers danced over the console.

"Salanin. And nitrated phenitol. Very nasty. Can't have been too much inside or the whole street would have gone up."

"You think the particle beam gun set it off?"

"No way. I've run through the films. The targetting was spot on. Maybe the presence of such raw energy could have upset a sophisticated timer but –" Norman shrugged.

"You think the guy in the white suit knew what he was carrying?"

"I don't know. He got away fast enough, didn't he? Did Spansky say where he met his contact?"

Jesse nodded. "And he gave us a pretty good description too. It's all here." He handed Norman a page from his notebook. As Norman fed the information into the computer, Jesse set about donning his skin-tight, frictionless, black motorcycle suit. By the time he had finished, a computer-realised portrait of a chubby faced man in his early fifties, with a broken nose, long sideburns and thin hair was staring back out of the screen. Jesse reached for his helmet.

"Now let's go and find out if our friend Spansky's telling the truth."

Norman ripped a computer print-out of the picture from the console and handed it to Jesse. "Go find him, Jesse," he urged. "This is a job for Street Hawk!"

After the usual dramatic flying exit from the camouflaged sliding doors of the secret Street Hawk hideaway, Jesse was soon cutting his way through the evening traffic on Freeway 91, with a full moon lighting up the sky above him and its splintered reflection winking and glittering in reply as he passed over the dark waters of the Los Angeles River. He kept it steady until he reached Clio's Bar, the small, dingy juke-joint where Spansky had met his man. He was slowly circling the block, checking out the terrain, when behind him the sudden sound of a burglar alarm was quickly followed by three sharp shots from a pistol. Jesse put on the air foils and skidded round to see two men running out of an all night chemist's shop, carrying small bags in one hand and guns in the other. Jesse cursed himself for not putting two and two together when he'd seen the young driver of the yellow Buick nervously pumping the engine as he waited outside the shop.

As the men dived through the window of the car Jesse called up his particle beam accelerator gun and the snub barrels clicked into position. "No dice, Jesse," Norman cut in. Jesse checked his targetting and saw why. An old lady, brushed aside by the fleeing thieves, stood on the sidewalk, her hands to her ears, screaming for all she was worth, while her husband stood in the road between Jesse and the car, angrily waving his walking stick at the car. The Buick lurched off, tyres smoking, smashed through a pile of garbage cans on the corner, sideswiped an abandoned Ford stacked up on bricks, then, as the sounds of the clattering bins resonated through the night, roared off down the street. Jesse accelerated to the corner, but before he reached it a black and white, sirens blaring, raced across the T-junction in hot pursuit.

"Leave it to them," Norman advised. "They'll nail those hoodlums for good."

Jesse eased off and set about following the cop car. "Sometimes a badge and a gun aren't enough."

Jesse stayed behind the patrol car as it squealed through the streets after the Buick. The police driver was good, but the crook in the Buick was crazier and more scared, and by a series of reckless, potentially catastrophic manoeuvres – including one where the diners at a pavement cafe were forced to jump to safety as the Buick ploughed through their tables, chairs and plates full of

abandoned food – he managed to keep the black and white behind.

Then the crooks in the back of the Buick knocked out the rear window and opened fire. The police car kept coming but one of the front tyres took a slug and as the driver desperately tried to speed up and ram the getaway car before he lost control, another slug shattered his windscreen and, momentarily blinded by the flying glass, he pulled the wheel too soon and the black and white bounced over a fire hydrant, spun across a deserted road and crashed backwards through the plate glass window of a fashion shop. As Jesse passed he saw the driver angrily beating the steering wheel with his fist.

Jesse quickly accelerated and within seconds his elegantly-styled, glimmering, glossy machine was travelling alongside the Buick.

"It's Street Fink!" yelled one of the crooks in the back.

"Waste that piece of junk!" yelled the other, levelling his gun. Jesse smiled to himself when he recognised the second hood as the man that Spansky had described. He pulled quickly ahead, slowed again, then took a quick left. When the Buick followed, he knew he was in business.

In a nerve-tingling game of cat and mouse, Jesse kept the crooks on his tail, always giving them the impression that with just a little bit of luck they could wipe him out. Then he took a swift right and found himself in a narrow alleyway. Ahead, in the darkness, the infra-red picked out some garbage cans stacked against a brick wall. Dead end. He shot down the alley and turned to face the Buick.

"We've got him, boys!" whooped the driver as the Buick entered the alley. Jesse sat motionless astride his highly polished partner and the Buick's headlights cast his eerie, outsize shadow on the wall behind. "Squash him flat!"

The driver put his foot to the floor. The engine thundered, the exhaust spat sparks through the blue smoke, and the yellow Buick sprang forward for the kill. When the front fender was less than a yard away, Jesse turned his throttle and cut in the compressed air vertical lift jets, and the multi-faceted motorcycle soared into the air. The driver of the Buick was still looking up, his mouth agape, when the car hit the wall with a devastating crunch. When Jesse landed behind the steaming wreck, suddenly the hunter had become the hunted, and the mouse had turned into a fully grown tiger.

Jesse dismounted. The driver was unconscious and the two thugs in the back were still dazed. Jesse dragged one out of the open door, ducked a roundhouse right and knocked him out with a left hook. He clipped the gun from the other's hand with a karate chop, grabbed him by the scruff of his jacket and pushed him up against the wall. In the distance he could hear the sound of approaching sirens. "Who's the man in the white suit?" Jesse demanded, tightening his hold.

The crook looked from side to side for help, his eyes glittering with fear. Jesse pushed him higher up the wall. "I-I-don't know!" he stammered. "He's some kook who pays me to pass on information."

"Where is he tonight?"

"He said something about the

Watts Towers! That's all I know! Now let me go, man – you're breaking my neck!"

Jesse let the thug slump to the floor, climbed aboard his masterpiece of motorcycle engineering, jet-jumped the arriving black and white, and asked Norman to activate hyperthrust. The Federal man complied and seconds later Jesse was on another jolting joyride through flashing lights and swiftly disappearing sounds. Norman cut out the hyperthrust as they came off the Harbour Freeway onto East 107th Street. A small crowd of boys and girls dancing round a huge radio on the pavement saw Jesse resume manual control and began shouting and waving.

"Hey, Street Hawk, my man! What's happening, brother?" called one.

"Looking for a grey haired man in a white suit," Jesse answered. The youth, still dancing, jerked his thumb in the direction of the three tapering towers made up of coloured pottery shards, sea shells, glass and pebbles all cemented to frames of scrap steel and baling wire. Jesse nodded and roared off towards the majestic 104 foot monument it had taken Simon Rodia 33 years to build.

"Jesse – to the right!" Norman's voice was urgent. Jesse hit the button, the air foils opened and the bike screeched to a halt. Down a dimly lit alley, two men were standing over the frail figure of the man in the white suit. He held one hand up to his head for protection and proffered them a smart attache case with the other.

"Don't touch that bag!" warned Jesse. The startled muggers turned, screwing their faces up in the sudden bright light. They looked puzzled until a soft rubber bullet hit one on the shoulder. He spun around, dropping his baseball bat, and was still holding his shoulder when they both ran off. The man in the white suit threw down his case and backed away down the alley from it.

"Why?" demanded Jesse.

The man's face grew angry at some bitter memory. "My wife!" he explained shrilly. "They killed her! She never harmed anyone and they killed her for a few measly dollars! They're all the same – the punks, the weirdoes, the muggers, the conmen, the thieves – they've polluted our streets for too long!"

"You can't just go round killing people. You need help."

The man put his hands to his face and fell to his knees, sobbing. "I . . . I know. I know . . . oh, Mary . . . oh . . ." He grabbed the case and held it to his chest.

When a black and white turned the corner along the street, Jesse rode forward and pulled the bag free from the man's grasp.

"Please . . . there's only four minutes to go." The old man's eyes were full of tears. "Tell the police what happened. I'll take care of this." Jesse zoomed off, Norman activated hyperthrust and as the magnificent mega-powered motorbike screamed along its computer-plotted course, the attaché case grew steadily hotter in Jesse's hands. Then suddenly they were at the harbour. Norman de-activated hyperthrust, Jesse skidded to a halt inches from the end of a pier and hurled the attaché case high into the air. At the top of its arc it blew up with an ear-blasting, cannon-like roar and as Jesse watched the blazing pieces fall sizzling into the black sea he felt a twinge in his heart for a frail old man in a white suit, sent mad with grief and rage and loneliness.

And then he turned his motorcycle round, gunned the engine, and hurried back to the streets.

Mayhem at the Museum

On the steps of the bombed-out museum, Commander Altobelli shook his head at Sandy, and held his hands in the air as he tried to halt the growing tide of questions from the horde of newsmen crowding round. He might as well have tried juggling sand. Without the cordon of uniformed officers to protect him, he would have been swamped by the sea of boom mikes, cameras, notebooks, tape recorders, and radios that threatened to drive him back into the still smouldering hulk of the once elegant building. He called once more for order as the questions came in fast and furious. Once again he was ignored.

"Is it true that the bombers left a ransom note?"

"Was the mayor's office given any warning of the attack?"

"What is the estimate of the damage caused?"

"Is there any link with the Anita Jay kidnapping?"

"When are the police going to turn up something new?"

"What is Officer Casey's condition?"

"Why did the fire preventions systems fail?"

"Is it true that Street Hawk is involved?"

The Commander winced. The last one hurt him the most. As if he didn't have enough trouble with the usual misery-go-round of stabbings, beatings, murders and robberies. Added to the list, in just one morning were the attempted homicide of a police officer, the suspected kidnapping of a movie mogul's daughter and the blowing up of the city's finest and most prestigious museum. And all the rabble out there with the cameras wanted to know was if they could get some quote on the motorcycle screwball who liked playing the Caped Crusader.

He called for quiet again, and when it didn't come he pushed Sandy to the fore. "You know how I hate this stuff," he hissed, looking for a way out through the ruins. "It's time to earn your corn. And if you play up that vigilante nutburger I'm turning in my badge."

Had Altobelli known what Street Hawk was up to at that moment, he might well have turned in his badge. While inventor Norman Tuttle was sitting in the command centre fretting about his three-million dollar all terrain pursuit vehicle, Jesse Mach had peeled off in his pursuit of H. J. Willet's yellow sports car as it entered a tunnel, raced over the mountain scrubland at speeds approaching 200 mph, and was now sitting by a billboard on the other side, gunning his engine and waiting for the car to reappear. With a little help from Bernie in the lab, the computer had fingered Willet as present at the scene of the Casey shooting. The traces of animal blood, sweat and sawdust found in the footprint at the officer's apartment had led Jesse to a slaughterhouse on the edge of town, where he saw that the manager, H. J. Willet, closely resembled – once you'd added a wig to cover his shiny bald head – the computer picture made up from all the eyewitness descriptions of a man seen acting suspiciously in the vicinity at the time of Casey's shooting. It had been quick work, even for a computer, and as Jesse straddled his superfast machine, he began to wonder if perhaps everything hadn't worked out just a little too pat. Tuttle's voice came on the headset to interrupt his thoughts.

"What are you doing out there – daydreaming?"

"Huh?" Jesse answered.

"The infra-red," Tuttle explained. "Willet's pulled a fast one inside the tunnel. The readings show the yellow sports is inside that furniture van that passed you nearly a minute ago. They must have loaded up while you were racing over that mountainside. I don't know why you want to risk such a beautiful machine like that –"

Jesse hit the accelerator and the spinning wheels churned up curtains of rock and sand as the bike roared down the side of the mountain and squealed through the oncoming traffic. He kicked in the thrusters to jump the concrete barriers between the lanes then weaved his way steadily through the stream of speeding vehicles towards the large furniture van carrying the suspect.

Inside the cab of that van, having driven his yellow sports car up the ramp then climbed through the hole into the passenger seat, H. J. Willet was beginning to sweat. He should never have taken a job so close to home in the first place. If the mob wanted to shut a snoopy cop up they should have done it themselves. Sure he was in the hole to them for more than enough green, but they should have respected his professionalism. They should have known he didn't like rush jobs. And when the cop had squirted that stuff in his eyes – it had been all he could do to get away alive. And now – now a cold

fear rocketed up from the base of his skull as he looked in the rear view mirror at the sinister black shape closing in on the lumbering van.

"You carrying?" he asked the driver.

"Under the seat."

Willet leaned forward and hauled out a 32 shot Uzi 9mm submachine gun from beneath his feet. He leaned out of the window and emptied the magazine at the pursuing supercycle. The slugs tore up the road and the bike swerved wildly, seemingly out of control, skidding out of sight behind the van. It took ten seconds for Willet to chance a smile and it froze on his face when Jesse appeared again, sliding out of the van's slipstream and edging alongside.

"This guy's not real!" Willet snarled, jamming another magazine into his machine gun. A rubber bullet roared from the speeding bike and sent it spinning from his hand into the road. The look of astonishment on Willet's face turned to abject fear when Jesse dropped back and activated his particle beam accelerator. The long blue flashes of energy snaked round the removal van as, inside, the tank of the yellow sports car began smoking and burst into flame. In the front, Willet and the driver were feeling groggy as the van's motor cut out and, with flames leaping from the back, it slewed off the road and ran downhill across the scrubland towards a steep ravine.

Jesse cut in the off-road suspension, accelerated alongside the bucking, blazing vehicle and reached up for the door to the cab. It was too high. Like a surfer catching a wave, he jumped to his knees, stood on the back of his bouncing bike and wrenched the door open. The driver fell out, rolled across the ground and lay groaning in the sand. Willet lay slumped across the seats. As the edge of the ravine came closer, Jesse grabbed the would-be killer by the back of his jacket and pulled him across the seat and out of the open door. He hit the brakes and the bike skidded to a halt as the runaway van left a fiery trail of debris, somersaulting down the ravine and exploding at the bottom, sending a thick black cloud rolling slowly up into the afternoon sunshine. Jesse checked the driver was alive and then kept the two crooks company until a pair of CHiPs arrived. One of them was producing his notebook when Norman activated the turbos. There was a howl of raw power and Jesse was out of sight before

the officer had put his paper and pencil away.

Back at the Command Centre Norman was expounding his theory.

"You're an engineer, not a detective." Jesse pointed out.

Norman winced. "I'm a Federal Agent, Mach – and kidnapping's a Federal offence. I've been tapping into a few systems – the museum's, its shipping agency's – I think they were using the museum as a front, smuggling narcotics inside foreign sculptures."

"Who's they?"

"The bad guys. They got a hold on one of the museum's agents – a man named Cook – when he got in too deep with gambling debts. The original deal was that he made a couple of runs for them but once he'd taken the bait they squeezed him till his ears bled. Our men had been waiting to see who was putting the pressure on Cook, and when they heard Anita Jay had been snatched they knew."

"I always suspected they trained you guys with comic books."

"I'm serious, Mach. Arnold Jay has been under observation for a long time. We've not been able to pin anything on him, but now it looks like Cook turned and a war's broken out. And when Casey got in the way, Jay sent Willet to nail him."

"You got any proof?"

Norman ran a tape showing a carved figure of a leopard being sawn in two. The hollow innards had been stuffed with plastic bags carrying white powder. He zoomed in on the small plaque at the bottom of the statue. The words DONATED BY ARNOLD JAY were clearly visible.

"What about Altobelli?" Jesse asked.

"His hands are tied. He hasn't got enough to go in for a bust and Jay's got some of the smartest lawyers in town."

"You know where Cook's holding Anita?"

Norman shook his head.

Jesse stood up and pulled the gleaming black helmet over his eyes. "Better strap yourself in, buddy," he warned. "This is a job for Street Hawk."

Minutes later the doors to the command centre slid open and the mighty motorcycle leapt over the piles of rubbish, landed skidding and squealing on the street, then raced off into the night with a full-throated roar.

The sun was getting low in the sky when Jesse reached Arnold Jay's mansion. Set back behind an orchard, it was surrounded by huge spiked walls and the wrought iron gate was carefully monitored by a closed circuit TV system. Inside the grounds Jesse could hear dogs snarling. He circled his

bike at a quiet corner of the estate, upped the revs and headed it straight for the wall. Just when it seemed he would crash head-on into the gleaming white 15 foot high structure he activated the compressed air jets and the magnificent motorbike soared into the air, clearing the razor sharp spikes topping the wall by inches, then landed heavily on its rear wheel by a flowing apple tree.

The dogs were on him at once. Three of them – Dobermanns – jumped up and down, snapping and snarling as the bike weaved through the orchard. Jesse set his particle accelerating beam onto stun and opened up. The vicious dogs howled as the crackling blue ray engulfed them, then fell to the floor unconscious. A similar fate met the squat man with the .44 Magnum who had come to investigate the noise, and by the time Jesse came screeching to a halt by Arnold Jay's pool two more of his armed thugs were lying dazed where they fell on the driveway. Arnold Jay looked up irritably from the inflatable chair he was sitting on. Jesse exploded the chair with a well aimed rubber bullet and when Arnold struggled spluttering to the surface of his pool the mysterious motorcyclist delivered his ultimatum.

"You tell me where Cook is or that water's going to get hot."

"I don't know anything. Please believe me."

"Casey's a friend of mine. You're going to pay for what happened to him. But if you've sent your goons to rescue your daughter a lot more people might get killed. I know Cook will have tried to make a deal, so spill it, fatso – where is he?"

"You're going to regret this, Mr Goody-Goody," said Jay, climbing out of the pool. "I've got friends in high places. I'm fireproof. But I love my daughter, and that souped-up skateboard might be just the thing to get her free. Cook's on the third floor of the Excelsior Hotel.. He said he's got my daughter there. My men are on their way to rub him out right now."

Jesse swerved away from the pool and sped back down the drive, cutting in the thrusters to jump the arriving black and white, then hanging on tight as, back at the controls, Norman went through the countdown to turbo activation. The bike reared up with the sudden surge of power and then everything seemed to blurr as the speedo on the top left hand corner of his visor reached 300 mph.

But, despite the awesome speed of his supercharged cycle, Jesse reached the Excelsior after Jay's thugs. As he slowed down in the hotel forecourt he heard a gunshot and the shattering of glass and

looked up to see two men wrestling for control of a pistol in a third floor window. He raced the bike up the forecourt steps and put the thrusters on maximum. The powerful jets shot the speeding cycle into the air, and he just had time to catch the look of disbelief on the fighting men's faces before he came smashing through the window in a shower of broken glass. He brought the bike under control with a sliding half turn that sent one thug diving for the bathroom and he then aimed his particle beam accelerator at the two men by the window. The blue ray fizzled and cracked and the men fell stunned to the floor. Another man ran out of the door as Jesse opened a cupboard and found Anita Jay tied up inside. He unfastened her bonds and checked she was unhurt. "I'm OK," she gasped, rubbing her wrists. "But Cook's escaped!"

"Not yet," corrected Jesse, gunning the motor and racing out of the room into the hotel corridor. Ahead of him the lift doors were hissing shut and the infra-red showed one man inside. The bike roared along the plush carpets, bumped down the marble staircase and when the lift doors hissed open again, Cook came face to face with the special agent cop and his magnificent, glistening motorcycle, its engine growling softly as it cut off all escape.

Two house detectives took Cook away and Jesse drove out of the open front door of the hotel and back to base.

At the press conference at police HQ that night, Jesse stood next to Commander Altobelli as he fielded a mixed bag of questions.

"Yes, we have a man under arrest for the shooting of Officer Casey. We are holding five others in connection with the museum bombing and the kidnapping."

The young reporter named Larry held up his pencil as he rose to his feet. "Is it true, Commander," he asked, "that Street Hawk was used on this case? That this vigilante is actually a part of the police force?"

"Next question," said Commander Altobelli curtly.

The young newsman pressed. "And is it not true that the use of such a sophisticated machine against the citizens of this country is in fact illegal, and against the constitution?"

"Is it true Street Hawk can fly?" asked another reporter.

"Is it true it can go underwater?" asked someone else.

"Can it talk?"

"Is it true the bike's driven by a super robot?"

As the questions poured in, once again Altobelli began to lose his cool. "This so-called vigilante is a menace to law and order," he protested, "and when we get hold of him he'll be charged with every traffic violation in the book. Now that's all I want to say on the subject, so if you will please direct any more questions to Officer Mach here, I'm sure he'll be able to deal with them for you." He gave Jesse an exasperated look as he made his way from the microphone. "After all," he continued quietly, "he's not done a stroke of work all day."

ACORNS, BAFFLES and CREEP

While Jesse Mach is an instinctive rider relying on skill, daring and intuition, Norman Tuttle is an altogether more pernickety type of person, fully aware of every aspect of a motorcycle's construction and performance as well as the terms to describe them. Here he has listed alphabetically a glossary of motorcycle words and phrases, and to show that he's not all work and no play – he's thrown in six false ones as well. Can you spot them?

1. Acorn nut – a hexagonal nut with a closed dome that improves appearance and prevents oil leaking along the threads.

2. Baffle – the plate used to deflect gases inside a silencer, or to prevent fuel sloshing around a half-full tank.

3. Creep – the slow deterioration of metal parts under stress at high temperatures, usually resulting in malfunction.

4. Delb spot – the point at which de-ionization occurs in the lateral thread of the cylinder bore.

5. E-clip – an external circlip whose three lugs give it the appearance of the letter E.

6. Ferrule – a small metal tube fixed around the ends of a Bowden outer cable to prevent fraying.

7. Grub screw – a blunt-ended screw that is usually used to retain a shaft.

8. Heptane – a paraffin hydrocarbon found in petrol. Its chemical composition is C_7H_{16}.

9. Iggle – measurement of rear wheel drift, and indicator of thickness of tread.

10. Joggle pin – a split-pin placed loosely in a hole so the continual movement will keep the hole clear.

11. Knurling – a criss-cross pattern on metal hand tools that helps give a non-slip grip.

12. Lampblack – a fine black soot produced when there is insufficient oxygen for complete combustion.

13. Monsford Circuit – an electrical system, named after its inventor, that lessens dehydration in the phlange.

14. Nadgery – a narrow, twisting trial section that tests balance at very slow speeds.

15. Omm link – small chain under the camshaft to minimise carburettor flooding.

16. Petroil – a mixture of petrol and oil that can be used as a two-stroke fuel.

17. Quad-u-loops – thick steel tubes fashioned in a series of hoops to transfer drive from manual to automatic.

18. Rectifier – a means of turning alternating current into direct current.

19. Shim stock – collective name for hard metal components such as washers, used to reduce play.

20. Tommy bar – a steel rod used mainly to turn box or socket spanners.

21. U-bolt – a curved steel rod, threaded at both ends, used mainly as a clamp.

22. Viscosity index – a scale revealing how much an oil thins when heated.

23. Wheelbase – the length of a machine between the front and rear spindles.

24. Xenon factor – trade description of damage caused by friction (usually through misuse) on the central carburettor tube.

25. Yoke – device connecting the stanchions of a telescopic fork with the steering column.

26. Zimmerman valve – named after its inventor, it is a disc valve common on many two-strokes.

ANSWERS: FALSE – 4, 9, 13, 15, 17, 24.

HIGH FLYERS

Although Norman Tuttle's majestic three-million dollar creation represents the state of motorcycle art, he is the first to admit that his wondrous gleaming monster owes several debts to the pioneer designers that went before him. In their day, some of the motorcycles mentioned below transcended the contemporary technology just as much as the Street Hawk machine does now, and they flew high enough above the rest to earn the right to be numbered among the brothers of the Hawk.

1. The Street Hawk motorcycle is an all-terrain pursuit vehicle equipped with infra-red cameras and audio sensors. Turbos give it hyperthrust capability and the dual control mode on the base computer means it seldom goes out of control. The compressed air vertical lift system, combined with the air foil brakes, enables it to execute back flips 30 feet in the air.

2. The Zenith Gradua brought a new dimension to hill climbing. In 1909 Zenith developed a system of expanding pulleys so that the rider, by furiously turning the long handle by the tank, could vary the gearing from 3:1 to around 8:1. This 1920 model was fitted with a JAP 750 cc side valve engine.

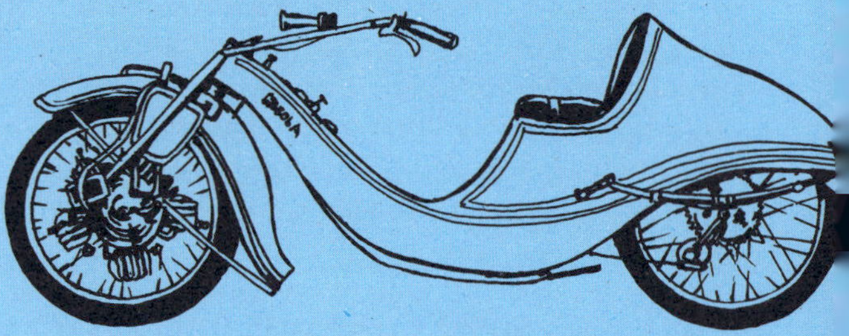

3. The Megola, built in Switzerland in 1922, belied its unusual appearance with an excellent performance record. Front wheel drive, with a five cylinder side valve engine that rotated with the wheel, the handling was good and the engine flexibility – 15 combustion strokes per wheel revolution – made the absence of a clutch unimportant. Racing models achieved speeds of 90 mph.

4. The Henderson Four was the creation of motorcycle visionary William Henderson, whose 1068 cc in-line sportster laid down the guidelines for a great American tradition. The first bike with a reliable clutch, it could top 60 mph, and although the peculiar front-mounted pillion seat shown here was abandoned after a year, the basic 1912 design was continued until 1931.

5. The 1926 Ace was Bill Henderson's legacy and revenge. When American Excelsior took over his own company in 1919, he developed the Ace, which went into production the same year. The Ace's 1266 cc engines were powerful enough to smash nearly every speed and endurance record in the book and it is a tragedy Henderson never lived to see the 1926 Ace, the luxurious realisation of everything he had started in 1919 – the year he died.

6. The BMW R69S hauled motorcycling into a new era. Fast, quiet, reliable, with superb brakes and smooth suspension, the BMW R69S brought a new sophistication to the general public of 1953. The 600 cc sports pictured here was a milestone of quality engineering and production, but commercial pressures proved too great and the line was discontinued in 1968 for a more economical model.

7. The Vincent Black Prince was another fine example of the post-war boom in motorcycle development. Still held in awe by enthusiasts everywhere, its 998 cc engine weighed 460 lb and gave a top speed of 120 mph and an average consumption of 65 mpg. Top class road holding and acceleration were matched by the sleek, futuristic lines and only the price (more than £400) stopped it reaching a wider audience.

8. The Aermacchi 250 Sports brought nippy 250 cc bikes back to the fore in the mid 1950s. Developed from a range of pushrod singles, they could easily top 100 mph and in 1962 the 246 Ala d'Oro racer was given the necessary accessories and sold as a road bike. Powerful, with good handling, the 250 Sports remains competitive today.

9. The Kawasaki Z900 was the first of Kawasaki's much heralded big fours and set the standards for the other Japanese superbikes produced later in the decade. With 12 valve, double overhead cam power units, these monsters easily reached speeds in excess of 130 mph, and only the less than perfect handling cast a shadow on an otherwise spotless reputation.

10. The Norton Commando Mk III marked the tragic end of an era. This 850 cc, 120 mph behemoth was Norton's last fling before the company faded away. Its Isolastic engine mounting system was the first really serious attempt to cut down the vibrations affecting most big twins, and by the time the Mk III appeared in 1975, the problem had been almost conquered. Sadly, it was already too late.

THE GRUDGE

Commander Altobelli leaned over his desk and handed the photograph to Jesse Mach. It showed an outstandingly beautiful girl in her early twenties, standing on tip-toe in a bathing costume and holding a beach ball above her head. The photograph was a black and white one that had been hand-painted in garish colours. Jesse recognised the girl as Lola Lamarr, film star, and once the biggest box office draw in the whole world.

"Look," Altobelli explained irritably, "maybe these days she's got a body like a sack full of laundry and a face like a bashed crab, but in this town she's still royalty. You got it?"

"I got it." Jesse nodded.

"Good. So when Lola Lamarr starts squawking about how she can't trust the police to protect her, people listen. That's why I want you on the show tonight."

"The show?"

"She's on some talk show on KBX. It'll be the usual stuff – how nobody's safe with all the scum on the streets, how somebody nailed a wreath to her front door, how she's forced to hire bodyguards because of the death threats –" Altobelli didn't even look up as a uniformed man placed a tray on his desk. There was a steaming cup of coffee and a plate covered with an upturned dish. "I want you there to put our case. And this afternoon I want you down on a film set with your arm around some star's shoulders – all in time for the evening papers."

Jesse didn't seem to hear. He was staring at the tray distractedly.

"Mach – have you gone deaf, or are you practising your dumb insolence?"

As if in answer, Jesse grabbed the tray with one hand and pushed over the desk with the other, knocking Altobelli and his chair onto their backs. He ran to the window, smashed the glass with his walking stick, checked there was nobody below, then hurled the tray out. Before it hit the ground it exploded, blowing in the windows on the ground floor in a fiery blast that left a pall of smoke slowly rising in the air.

Jesse helped Altobelli to his feet and began picking up the papers that had spilled from the upturned desk.

"The guy's uniform," Jesse explained, as outside the sirens joined the sounds of running feet and shouted orders. "It was NYPD. And those strange gloves he was wearing – they weren't police issue. And when I saw the yellow smoke coming from under the plate – I didn't figure it was the mustard on the salami." Jesse righted the desk, rapped the bottom of the sheaf of papers on

the corner, and handed them to Altobelli.

"Not bad for an ex-motorcycle cop," he said grudgingly. "I don't suppose you got a look at his face?" Jesse shook his head. "All right then," the commander continued. "I don't think there's anything more to keep you, is there?"

Jesse smiled and headed for the door. He had just opened it when Altobelli's voice stopped him.

"Oh, Mach –"

"Yeah?"

"Make sure you send a glazier up before you go, huh?" The two men nodded and Jesse set out for tinsel town.

An hour later, on a sound stage on a back lot, Jesse was talking to veteran film director Jason Stang beside a huge tank containing detailed miniatures of Japanese and American warships.

"Sure," Stang smiled, admiring the scene. "I know a lot of people who'd like Lola Lamarr dead. Her heart would break a scalpel and her tongue could cut through stone."

"Have you ever worked with her?" Jesse asked.

A cloud crossed Stang's features. "Once. It was not a positive experience."

"You want to tell me about it?"

"I don't suppose it will do any harm," shrugged Stang, stepping back from the tank and offering Jesse a seat. "There's going to be the mother and father of a ruckus about it anyway. It was back in '55. The film was called *Moon Bride*."

Jesse's face showed no sign of recognition. Stang continued wearily. "It's no wonder you haven't heard of it. It was never released. There was an accident on the set – some people got killed – and the studio sat on the whole thing. But things are different now. *Moon Bride* would have been the first sword 'n' sorcery film, and although it never got finished, we got some of the best ever SFX sequences in the can. Ghosts, monsters, earthquakes – stuff that would cost billions today. The people who now own the rights reckon that an old scandal will be good for business and they're planning to build round the effects, shoot a few new scenes – maybe top and tail it with Lola as she is today – you've got to admit –"

Suddenly Stang's eyes grew wide and his voice changed to a snarl. "Hey, you! Leave that switch alone!"

Stang's warning went unheeded. A switch was thrown, powerful motors started up, and the warships in the tank went into action. Tiny guns blazed, water spouts erupted, miniature aircraft carriers burst into flames, and black smoke drifted in thick clouds across the surface of the tank. The sound set was suddenly full of people running round and shouting at each other, waving their arms and jumping up and down, pointing fingers, pulling hair, accusing and abusing, adding further mayhem to the already chaotic scene. As a stricken destroyer slipped below the water line, Jesse turned to Stang and felt a cold knot of fear tighten in his stomach. The grizzled director sat slumped in his chair, his hand clutching the dark red stain slowly spreading across his stomach.

That night, with Stang unconscious in hospital and a torrid TV grilling thankfully behind him, Jesse cruised the street on his glossy, low-slung, hyperpowered supercycle, worrying at the problem like a dog at a bone. After Stang had been taken away in an ambulance the studio had been extremely helpful, and Jesse had left Norman with a few reels of film and a whole wealth of new information to work on. He felt sure the key to the mystery was the unfinished *Moon Bride*, but if he was right, where did that leave Altobelli? The commander couldn't have been much more than a rookie when the film was first made. And why had –

"Bad news, Jesse," Norman's worried voice cut in. "Lola Lamarr got snatched on the way back from the studio. Red Caddy jumped a roadblock at Crown Vista and Compton."

"I'm on my way."

Jesse gunned the engine of his sleek speedster and as the speedo inside his helmet rose towards the 200 mph mark, he listened to Norman's voice coolly completing the countdown to hyperthrust. And then the turbos spat flame, the engines howled, and his power packed metal partner exploded into action, eating up the road so fast that Jesse was only dimly aware of the myriad scenes flashing by, as night time LA was reduced to a brilliant flurry of streaking light and staccato sound. Man and machine seemed to merge and Jesse got a hint of what it must be like to enter another dimension as he thrilled to the pace and precision of Norman's computer plotted course.

"Dead ahead," said Norman, cutting out the hyperthrust.

Jesse slowed as he pulled alongside the red Caddy. Inside, a grey-haired man, his face a mask of venomous rage, held the steering wheel with one gloved hand as the other clutched the wrist of the struggling Lola Lamarr. He screeched an unintelligible curse at Jesse as they crossed the LA river and tugged hard on the wheel, violently swerving the Caddy in an attempt to force the jet black machine and its rider off the bridge. Jesse cut in the compressed air vertical lift jets, the speeding bike hissed angrily upwards, and the Caddy skidded below, tearing into the bridge's railings, crushing the front of the car and slewing it round. By the time Jesse had landed and turned, the man had dragged Lola from the wreck and was standing on the parapet, ready to jump. Jesse hesitated. For once, the amazing array of weaponry on his dynamic machine was useless. He dismounted and walked slowly towards them.

"Take it easy," he said softly. "We can work something out."

The man laughed contemptuously. A sneer was forming on his lips when Lola suddenly stamped on his foot and dug her elbow into his stomach. The man howled and let her go, then stood tottering on the parapet as Lola jumped clear. When the man started falling backwards, Jesse lunged forward and grabbed his hand. It felt cold and hard, and although he kept it firmly in his grasp, the man continued falling, the empty arm of his coat fluttering behind him as he dropped, his chilling, high-pitched laugh rising vengefully until he hit the black waters below. There was a dull splash, faint ripples slid out in the darkness, then only Lola's muted sobbing and the wrecked Caddy bore witness to the fact that the man had ever been there at all.

Back in the secret Street Hawk command centre, Norman ran some unspliced takes from *Moon Bride* while Jesse filled him in with what Lola had told him.

"Seems he had a part in *Moon Bride*," Jesse explained. "He was there when the accident happened."

"What's all this got to do with Altobelli?" asked Norman. On the screen, a lavish banquet in a mediaeval castle was about to begin.

"Altobelli had a tip that one of the cameramen on the film had been involved in a hit and run. He arrived to question him in the middle of the take. The camera was meant to follow Lola through a crowd of conjurors and magicians. When the cameraman saw Altobelli, he panicked. Lola didn't like it and turned on him. A fight

started. Altobelli and Stang tried to stop her, but the cameraman fell off the boom and the camera ran out of control. Some people got knocked down. A fire broke out. Four people – including the cameraman – were killed. There!" Jesse pointed to the screen. "Run that bit again."

Norman re-wound the film and rolled it again in slow motion. It showed the banquet scene, where Lola Lamarr, in a flowing silk dress, was laughingly picking her way through a crowd of tumblers, clowns, magicians, conjurors and minstrels. Suddenly the smile dropped from Lola's face. She turned angrily and advanced towards the camera. The screen went dark. Then Stang could be seen trying to restrain Lola. They fell to the ground and the camera tilted crazily, panning along a length of collapsing scaffolding, taking in a startled minstrel diving for cover, a juggler stumbling and falling backwards, and, as the scaffolding came crashing down, a single white dove that fluttered from the sleeve of a frightened magician who held up his arms in a vain and hopeless attempt to protect himself.

"That's him!" said Jesse. Norman stopped the film and went through the papers the studio had given Jesse.

"Bruce Bodene. Also known as The Mysterious Marvel." Norman shook his head sadly. "Lost an arm." He ran Bodene's name through the computer files. "Arrested in May 1957 for arson at the same studios. Some dispute over compensation. Freed on bail and re-arrested the next day for damaging studio equipment. Took an axe to Lola Lamarr's caravan. Detained for psychiatric observation. Frequent outbursts of violence. Finally released in March this year."

"Any address?" asked Jesse.

Norman nodded, and Jesse reached for his helmet.

"The man fell off the bridge!" Norman reminded him.

Jesse grinned. "I got a gut feeling –"

"I know, I know," groaned Norman. "And what chance has logic, reason, and a million dollars worth of computer equipment against an ex-chippie's hunch?"

The camouflaged doors of the command centre slid open, splitting the painting of the globe, and the still of the night was rudely shattered by a blasting fanfare of booming engines as the world's most advanced motorcycle flew from its lair and sailed over the abandoned crates and bags of rubbish. The hydraulic suspension system took the sting out of the landing, and within seconds Jesse was on the open road, opening the throttle and watching the speedo inside his helmet rise to 150 mph. He reached Bodene's address in

less than five minutes.

Jesse felt uneasy as he climbed the stairs. Somewhere in the building a heated argument was taking place in a language he couldn't recognise. He stopped at Bodene's door and listened. There was no sound. He looked at the floor and saw a thin trickle of water snaking its way under the door. He stepped back and kicked the door open.

There was nobody in the room. A pile of wet clothing lay discarded by the door. A single cupboard stood by the unmade bed, its door hanging open. Jesse's heart quickened when he saw the picture of Altobelli, pinned to the inside of the door with a carving knife. He ran downstairs, climbed back on his bike, opened the throttle and headed straight for the commander's house.

"He's not home, Jesse," Norman informed him. "I've been in touch with the station. He and Sandy are having a meet with some community leaders at the Rio Antonio Hotel."

"Where's that?" asked Jesse testily.

"It's up in the mountains. Hang on and I'll take you there."

Norman went through the countdown then engaged hyperthrust. For a brief second, as the turbos flared and the blaring black beast beneath him blasted forward, Jesse felt like his arms were being pulled from their sockets, and when the turbulence subsided, he took up the hyperthrust position, and his blood began racing with joyous excitement. His spirit kept rising with the numbers on the speedo, and by the time he hit the 300 mph mark and entered the barrelling kaleidoscope of rocketing light and sound, his heart was pumping wildly and he was gripped by a swelling, jubilant feeling of freedom and exhilaration. He was almost sorry when Norman cut out hyperthrust and returned him to manual.

At the San Antonio Hotel, Jesse's spirits slumped still further. Broken glass covered the forecourt and several people were walking around in a daze. Jesse stopped by a tall man in an orange t-shirt who was holding a paper towel to a cut on his head. "What happened?" he asked.

"You're asking me? My head feels like someone's opened an aviary in there. My hands won't stop shaking. My ears feel like –"

"There was a bomb," explained a man in a dinner suit, coming out of the foyer. "And then a madman kidnapped the girl. The commander went after them."

"Which way did they go?"

The man pointed towards the mountains and Jesse gunned the throttle.

"Hold it, Jesse," urged Norman from the command centre as he studied the screen. "What's that on the floor?" He zoomed in on a dark puddle on the carpet.

Jesse walked over with the man in the suit and knelt down. "It's brake fluid, Norm," he reported, then looked up at the man in the suit. "Is this where the commander left his car?"

"I think so."

"That's all we need," Jesse grumbled. He was still shaking his head when he remounted the bike, hit the throttle and screeched off along the mountain road.

It took Jesse around seven minutes to catch up with Altobelli. By that time the road had ceased rising and the commander was making his way down a tortuous series of narrow S-bends, gathering speed all the time. On the winding road below them Jesse could make out the headlights of another car. He cruised up alongside.

"Get away from me!" yelled Altobelli, spinning the wheel and squealing round a tight bend.

Jesse kept close. "Your brakes!" he shouted. "He's cut your brakeline!"

"So what?" Altobelli ignored the next corner, taking a short cut down the steep, shale covered slope. Jesse stayed with him as the commander's car bucked and bounced over the rough ground then smashed back onto the road with such momentum that only Altobelli's superb driving skills kept it from going over the edge of a cliff.

Jesse smiled as he came up alongside again. "Try and run her up against the cliff wall," he advised.

Altobelli scowled. "Put an egg in a sock and beat it." There were now only two bends between Altobelli's car and Bodene's. "I'm going to crush that crazy creep!" Suddenly he swung the wheel again and his battered car slid off the road and began bumping down the mountainside, kicking up dirt as the commander made a last desperate effort to ram Bodene's car.

Jesse could see he wasn't going to make it. Bodene was travelling too fast and the commander was losing control. And if the commander missed Bodene he was on a one-way ride to oblivion. Jesse gunned the engines and raced ahead of Altobelli, bringing up the particle beam guns and trying to target Bodene's car. He hit the firing button as he rode and Bodene's care began to shake and slow down, and then the engine cut out, the brakes seized up and Sandy and her captor fell unconscious across the seats. Altobelli's thundering, jumping limo, howling downhill like a runaway train, glanced off a large boulder and briefly left the ground before it ploughed into the back of Bodene's stationary vehicle. The front windscreen smashed and the bonnet flew up, but the commander was out of the car before it had stopped bouncing. He cuffed Bodene to the car door, and dragged Sandy out and stood her up. Jesse was turning to go when he heard Altobelli speak.

"Sorry I took so long," he explained to Sandy. "But that Street Hawk was hanging around with his stupid ray gun. The trigger happy fool nearly made me miss you!"

TRIP
MPH
LOW
HI
lbs
in
V